Ordinary to Extraordinary

Advance Praise

"I wish I had this book at the start of my career. I was always on the go and perpetually short of time. A set of simple to follow principles would have been a godsend! Fortunately, Gary Josephson, a successful surgeon and leader, articulates seven principles to help persons early in their careers (and others) overcome adversity and accelerate their journey to lifelong success and satisfaction. Designed as a quick read, I found its simplicity and wisdom to be ideal for the person who is short on time but unsure of how to move from an ordinary existence into an extraordinary life."

—R. Kevin Grigsby, MSW, DSW, Senior Director, Member Organizational Development, Association of American Medical Colleges (AAMC), Washington, DC

"A true delight! I felt cheered on and encouraged throughout this entire read. Dr. Josephson shares his experiences and insight in such an uplifting way, you can't help but want to glean more positivity from this great life guide, which addresses sensitive decisions we all make; money management issues, living healthy—even dating advice! Despite all I have seen in nearly 30 years as a journalist, I'll be rereading *O2E* the next time life throws me a curve ball!"

—Joy Purdy, News Anchor, WJXT News4 Jax

"Dr. Gary Josephson does an excellent job capturing the essence of what I believe many of us think about but sometimes have trouble putting into practice, particularly in challenging times—how to live your best life, every day. Dr. Josephson says it best in two quotes that describe the path toward a successful life and our impact on our community: 'Surrounding yourself with people who wish to make a positive impact on others is what day-to-day community building is about' as well as 'It's never too late to begin the journey and the path has the power to change anyone.' I thoroughly enjoyed his book and highly recommend it. As you read his personal stories and reflect on his seven powerful principles you recognize what you CAN control. Dr. Josephson reminds us that it's not too late, even in unprecedented times, to achieve a better total quality of life for ourselves and others. We must believe we have choices and with an 'attitude of gratitude' we can turn our vision of success into reality. He offers a practical approach, in a concise yet comprehensive way, with tips that will work for anyone to reach the goal of a well-lived life."

—**Charlotte F. Hughes**, CEO & Co-Founder,
Entrepreneur, Inclusive Leaders Group

". . . Dr. Josephson's seven principles in the hands of the diligent steward will help move one's life from ordinary to extraordinary starting with the power of attitude and ending with generosity. Food for the most fit . . . a must read for the initiate who wants to take life to the mountaintop of purpose and meaning."

—**Scott Wooten**, Executive Vice President/CFO,
Strategy and Finance, Baptist Health Jacksonville

"Great read. . . If anyone were to follow these seven steps, life success and fulfillment are almost guaranteed."

—**Craig Savage**, Partner, Wealth Advisor Private Wealth
Management Group, William Blair & Company

"Who wouldn't want a boost for success? Dr. Gary Josephson shares seven principles that he has found helpful in his successful life and others will too. The principles are down to earth and long lasting, no matter where you are along the journey. Each principle ends with tips and, to appease any skeptic, includes facts supporting the validity of the principle. The importance of synergy of the principles results in an exceptionally strong finish."

—**Pamela S. Chally, PhD**, Interim President,
University of North Florida

"As an accomplished and highly respected physician, Gary Josephson has directly impacted the health and well-being of countless people. Artfully described in *Ordinary to Extraordinary*, Dr. Josephson provides insight into the fundamental principles that have fueled his career success and more fundamentally his life success. Through relatable examples and practical tips, the seven principles for life success provide a thought-provoking framework to unlocking a more fulfilling life."

—**Chuck Divita**, GuideWell and Florida Blue,
Executive Vice President of Commercial Markets

"*Ordinary to Extraordinary* was a great read. I totally loved it. The seven principles were spot on for anyone yearning for a boost to success. Dr. Josephson provides a rare combination of thought-provoking principles and practical guidance. Together these form a recipe for success that anyone can follow. From the first principle of positive attitude to the last principle of living a benevolent life, the seven principles will help you to live a purpose-driven life journey. I enjoyed it so much, I am having my children read it!"

—**Russ Thomas**, Chief Executive Officer, Availity, LLC

"If you are looking for an easy to read and captivating guide to life success, then *Ordinary to Extraordinary: Seven Principles for Life Success* is the book for you. Whether you are hoping to be promoted, transform yourself as an innovator or improve your personal relationships, the principles outlined in this book will help you get there. Dr. Josephson brings a personal and unique perspective to the scientific and historical literature on how to be successful. Being fortunate to be in the graduating class that heard Dr. Josephson's commencement address, I and many of my classmates and our parents were intrigued and inspired by his seven principles. He has now shared them in a book with great examples for everyone interested to enjoy."

—**Spencer F. Weintraub, MD**, Resident Physician, Department of Medicine, North Shore University Hospital and Long Island Jewish Medical Center

"*Ordinary to Extraordinary: Seven Principles for Life Success* does a masterful job sorting through the complexities of everyday life to provide clarity on achieving success. Dr. Josephson delivers powerful and compelling guidance regarding the rationale for applying key tactics for success in each of the seven principles. Readers wishing to enhance their personal potential for success will be richly rewarded no matter their stage in life. Truly a wonderful read …"

—**Kent Thielen, MD**, Vice President Mayo Clinic, CEO Mayo Clinic Florida Operations

"Dr. Josephson's book provides a framework for action that anyone can implement to achieve greater success. The easy to read and cleverly formatted book shares seven principles designed to be incorporated together for more happiness, prosperity, and self-sustainability. I found each principle clear and effectively communicated. This book was perfect for someone like me who doesn't have a lot of time to read but wants to continue to grow personally and professionally."

—**Keli Coughlin Joyce**, CEO, Tom Coughlin Jay Fund

"*Ordinary to Extraordinary: Seven Principles for Life Success* is a truly extraordinary inspirational guide that can absolutely change your personal and business lives! As a lifelong successful entrepreneur, I fully recognize the importance and brilliance of his writings and actually employ many of his guiding principles in my day-to-day life. Although weighty, it is an easy and compelling read that includes concrete action one can take to enrich their personal and business lives. I … will recommend it to all of my employees and colleagues!"

—Jack Hanania Sr.,
Founder of Hanania Automotive Group

ORDINARY TO
EXTRAORDINARY

Seven Principles
for Life Success

GARY JOSEPHSON, MD MBA

NEW YORK

LONDON • NASHVILLE • MELBOURNE • VANCOUVER

Ordinary to Extraordinary

Seven Principles for Life Success

Published in New York, New York, by Morgan James Publishing. Morgan James is a trademark of Morgan James, LLC. www.MorganJamesPublishing.com

Proudly distributed by Ingram Publisher Services.

Scripture taken from the New King James Version®. Copyright © 1982 by Thomas Nelson. Used by permission. All rights reserved.

Morgan James BOGO™

A **FREE** ebook edition is available for you or a friend with the purchase of this print book.

CLEARLY SIGN YOUR NAME ABOVE

Instructions to claim your free ebook edition:
1. Visit MorganJamesBOGO.com
2. Sign your name CLEARLY in the space above
3. Complete the form and submit a photo of this entire page
4. You or your friend can download the ebook to your preferred device

ISBN 9781631958199 paperback
ISBN 9781631958205 ebook
Library of Congress Control Number: 2021949723

Cover Design by:
Megan Dillon
megan@creativeninjadesigns.com

Interior Design by:
Christopher Kirk
www.GFSstudio.com

Morgan James is a proud partner of Habitat for Humanity Peninsula and Greater Williamsburg. Partners in building since 2006.

Get involved today! Visit MorganJamesPublishing.com/giving-back

To my beautiful wife, Patricia:
The single most important decision one can make in their life is the person they decide to spend their life with. You are my guiding light and inspiration, my strength, balance, and support, my love, my friend, and my soul mate. You have brought so much meaning to my life. I am truly blessed. I love you.

To my children, Samantha and Grayson:
You have taught me the depth to which a child could be loved. I enjoy watching you both grow and exemplify ordinary to extraordinary. I am so proud of both of you. I give you all my love.

Contents

Acknowledgments

I am grateful and have been blessed with getting to know so many wonderful people throughout the course of my life that I do not even know where to begin with my acknowledgments. But here I go. Thank you to my teachers and mentors, who have given me the education and skills to care for my patients and manage and lead thoughtfully for the roles and responsibilities that I have been selected to perform. And thank you to my patients and their parents, who have given me permission, the opportunity, and the privilege to practice my trade and care for them the best way I know how.

I want to thank those whose quotes I used throughout the book as these words of wisdom inspire many and offer great contribution recognizing the human value in seizing opportunities. I want to also thank those who were the essence of the stories I shared that exemplified each principle.

Thank you to all my friends and those acquaintances who have enlightened me and with whom I have been privileged to share long-term friendships or short-term learnings. I would like to express my deepest gratitude to the many people who have been a source of support, inspired my drive over the years, and were instrumental in my steadfastness to complete this book. Amongst these individuals who know who they are, I would like to offer special mention by name to Dr. Paul Levine, Dr. Kenneth Grundfast, Dr. Jim Reilly, Dr. Charles Gross, Brian Kannard, Josephine Carubia, Michael Boots, Marybeth Kimball, Steven Heller, Dr. Steven Feit, Dr. Yosef Krespi, Dr. Charles Green (in memory), and my colleagues and coworkers at my current and former institutions. Also, I want to take a moment to thank my publisher, Morgan James Publishing, for bringing my book to life.

I would be remiss if I did not offer a thank you to my life contributors and inspirers in my family. I especially want to recognize my father and mother, Stanley (in memory) and Sheila Josephson, and my in-laws, Emilio and Clara (in memory) Solo, my siblings and their families with special recognition during the writing of this book to my sister, Amy, and my sister-in-law and brother-in-law, Helena and Frank, and their children, Christina and Elizabeth, for their unwavering kindness. I would like to thank my wife, Patricia, who has been my greatest source of support, and to my two children, Samantha and Grayson, who are a great inspiration and offer me much pride.

And last but not least, I want to offer special thanks in advance to all those who read this book on their quest to take their life from ordinary to extraordinary.

With much appreciation and many thanks, I am forever grateful.

"Hardship often prepares an ordinary person for an extraordinary destiny."

C.S. Lewis,
November 29, 1898–November 22, 1963,
British writer and lay theologian.

Preface

Countless books, articles, and seminars offer steps, secrets, and strategies for success, but millions are still thirsting for the wellspring of a fulfilling life. When someone with perceived success is encountered, we often ask how he or she does it. What if a simple set of rules or principles performed correctly could enhance these opportunities, increase well-being, and bestow that success we long for? Would we want to share this with our family, friends, and others so they could enjoy this richness? Of course we would! Many life events have inspired my drive, hard work, and enthusiasm and have given me a modicum of success. Being blessed with many experiences and the opportunity to learn from them has granted me a more fulfilling life enriched by those I have touched or who have influenced me. My goal is to offer not rules or recipes but a secure foundation of seven principles in a quick, easy read that can reach many and have a great impact. The audience for this book is anyone of any age yearning for a boost toward success and satisfaction: high school and college graduates entering the workforce (and their parents), young professionals seeking new challenges, and those who want to refresh their motivation and potential. While simple to follow, these principles can change an ordinary existence into an extraordinary life, just as they did for me.

Introduction

*"A story has no beginning or end: arbitrarily one
chooses that moment of experience from which to look
back
or from which to look ahead."*
Graham Greene, 1904–1991,
English novelist whose work focused on
international politics and espionage

On a warm Saturday in May, I sat on the podium with professors of the sciences, the dean, and other invited faculty. I was waiting for my turn in the lineup of speeches at the commencement ceremony for the graduating class of my undergraduate alma mater. Six months earlier, I had received a phone call from the alumni director inviting me to be the commencement speaker for this graduating class. I was perplexed by the call and wondered aloud, "Why me?"

He responded, "We like to invite alumni who have made a great contribution in their path to success."

What makes me the expert on this subject matter? I do not have formal training on the topic. But as I prepared my first commencement address, I realized that the road I have traveled has been notable to others as a path of success.

My journey from humble beginnings to extraordinary success began in a middle-class family on Long Island. I was the youngest of four children, and neither of my parents had completed a college education. I was bullied throughout most of elementary school, and that tormented me during much of my early life. It also influenced the choice I made to pursue a career as a child healthcare provider and advocate. I graduated from high school but was not at the top of my class. The only letters I ever wore on my jacket were my own initials. I experienced a life setback with an accidental electrical injury that required physical therapy, a positive attitude, and massive determination to keep me focused on my lifelong dream of becoming a surgeon.

I have learned from my experiences, celebrated failure as an educational opportunity, and taken advantage of all that life has to offer. My professional career has led me to leadership and service as a pediatric otolaryngologist-head and neck surgeon and chief medical officer. I run a financially substantial part of operations for one of the most prestigious and altruistic pediatric healthcare institutions in this country. On the personal side, I have been blessed with a wonderful marriage of more than twenty years, two healthy, respectful, well-intentioned children, and a balanced life.

So why write this book? People define and measure success in many ways. When I ponder the definition of life success, I believe it to be happiness, prosperity, and self-sustainability through and to the end of one's life. The discipline necessary to attain this starts first with understanding what it takes to achieve that end point. It is never too late to begin the journey and the path has the power to change anyone.

The world is evolving, as it always has, and continues to change. People are living longer than ever before and the responsibility for caring for that longevity has shifted to the individual. Career employment with a single employer is no longer the norm. Defined pension plans, plans for long-term employees that guarantee retirement income, are the exception rather than the rule. Few are the number of people that stay at a single employer for their entire career. It has now become more common for people to change career opportunities several times in their lifetime. Consumerism leads the way, which changes the dynamics by which we live. Loan requirements are more stringent, debt has increased, and personal financial accountability is expected. When we think of success, we recognize obstacles and hope to create the yellow brick road around them. Here is the rub. There is a general disconnect of the ingredients needed to reach these goals. We have our desire as a society to want and obtain immediate gratification. This may be due to a lack of the fundamental knowledge to create a long-term sustainable plan and have patience. Unfortunately, rather than supporting and teaching the way, businesses, government, and communities have become enablers. Without appropriate discipline and restraint, there are numerous ways to make poor choices and spiral into trouble. It is difficult to get back on track once people have fallen prey to their own poor decisions. A simple example is debt. A single maxed-out credit card can start a chain reaction that saps our financial and mental stability. The reality is, we need to live and enjoy today, and if we do that responsibly, we can have both the enjoyments we desire and the success of long-term self-sustainability well into our retirement years.

My love of teaching, coaching, and mentoring has given me great joy. Observing people contribute and lead while reaching their full potential and positively impacting our society could not be more rewarding. This is the essence of my decision to share this simple set of principles that, if adopted, can create the ability to enjoy much success in life. Living by these seven principles is a way of life for me. The destination thus far has not been intentional but has been enjoyed through a journey with discipline, determination, and hard work. If I can do it, then with the same enthusiasm and dedication, you too can enjoy lifetime success.

Ordinary to Extraordinary is a fundamental guide for anyone, even from the most humble or difficult background, to achieve sustainable success and fulfillment. Each principle individually offers success, but all seven practiced together become much more powerful.

Read, do, watch, and see!

Matters of Fact

Definitions of Success:

"1) Degree or measure of succeeding, 2) favorable or desired outcome, 3) the attainment of wealth, favor, or eminence." Merriam-Webster dictionary

"1) the favorable or prosperous termination of attempts or endeavors; the accomplishment of one's goals, 2) the attainment of wealth, position, honors, or the like." Dictionary.com

"1) the achieving of the results wanted or hoped for, 2) something that achieves positive results." Cambridge dictionary

PRINCIPLE ONE:

attitude, Attitude, ATTITUDE!

Create, choose, and control your attitude.

"Attitude is a little thing that makes a big difference."
Winston Churchill, 1874–1965,
British Prime Minister during World War II,
army officer, and writer.

Positivity always beats negativity! Attitude is a psychological and emotional behavior that profoundly affects our person internally and how we are perceived by our external environment. Our general attitude and demeanor are formed from a culmination of our experiences, good and bad. Understandably, someone who has faced many challenges in life may have a pessimistic outlook. Or maybe it is an innate trait of who they are; however, that does not mean this cannot be changed or modified to serve them well. Why? Because when we speak about attitude, we are talking about a personal choice. A positive or negative attitude is up to us.

Having a positive attitude is the psychological and emotional commitment to programming our minds to positivity. There is an entire discipline or field of study called "positive psychology." The term was first coined by Abraham Maslow in the 1950s to call for a more balanced view of human nature or, more specifically, human potentialities. Positive psychology was later popularized in 2002 by psychologist Martin Seligman from the University of Pennsylvania. It is well studied as it has caught significant attention in the field of psychology for more than a decade and is germane to our understanding of how optimism and a positive attitude offer success. The research has been compelling in its impact on our well-being internally and on how we are perceived externally. One example of the research done by Seligman studied the relationship between positive attitudes and success in sales. Seligman discovered that, at MetLife Insurance Company, agents who scored in the top half for optimism sold 37 percent more than those in the more pessimistic bottom half. He also noted that those agents in the top 10 percent for optimism sold 88 percent more than those who ranked in the most pessimistic 10 percent. That is notable for sure.

When I consider the attributes one must pursue in order to create a positive attitude, a positive demeanor, creativity, and a willingness to take on some risk in your pursuits—along with hard work, discipline, and determination to reach your goals—are essential. This is done through controlling your personal psyche, having emotional intelligence (self-awareness, along with the willingness to listen and modify our behaviors when necessary), and cultivating masterful communication skills to allow yourself to be an influencer and leader; it is done by putting a smile on your face, being cheerful, offering positive greetings around others, and looking at the bright side of life. My first encounter on this journey began when I was seven years of age. I lived about a mile from my elementary school and walked to and from school every day. One rainy day, I grabbed my windbreaker and was about to run out the door when my mother challenged me.

"Where are you going?"

"To school, of course," I replied.

"You do realize it is raining and that you *cannot* go to school in that windbreaker. You will be soaked by the time you get to school."

My mother proceeded to take a bright yellow slicker out of the closet along with black galoshes and a yellow rubber hat, all hand-me-downs from my older siblings.

"You will wear this to stay dry," she said.

"I can't wear that!" I insisted.

"Why not?"

"Because I will get beat up!"

My mother knelt, looked me in the eyes, and with her quiet strength, she said, "Gary, wear the coat, stay dry, and be a leader, not a follower."

Her words went right through me like a supercharge of electricity. I wore that yellow raincoat. I did *not* get beat up that day, but one bigger kid teased me, and more vicious bullying would continue from him for years. But for me, that yellow raincoat became the symbol of a turning point in how I thought about myself. I realized that I wanted to be a leader and that I *would* have a positive attitude. Yellow became my favorite color, and rain to me was liquid sunshine—a sign of optimism. From that day forward, whenever someone told me that I could not achieve something, I worked harder to prove that I could. I would do things that I knew were right and not be influenced by my peers. I would be a self-thinker with strong ethics and high integrity. Of course, I would still consider the thoughts and ideas of others, but ultimately my decisions would be mine, and I would own them. Attitude is first among the seven principles that created opportunities allowing me to choose the road that I would travel in life.

It is easy to say I will have a positive attitude. Some variables can affect our ability to display this behavior. One of the most impactful variables is our psyche. Take a moment to think of something that has recently occurred that made you feel good. Maybe your favorite sports team won a game; maybe you got positive feedback from someone, your child won an award at school, or you invested in a stock that has done well. When you think of these things, consider how they made you feel. I am sure you felt happy and had a sense of well-being. Just the same, negative things can bring us down. Fortunately, we do have control of our minds. Let's say we play a recreational sport with friends and our team loses the game. We do not have control of winning or losing the game. We do have the ability to control how that can make us feel or act. Rather than taking the position of "we lost and our team is terrible," a positive outlook would be that we enjoyed time with friends, received a nice dose of exercise, and learned skills that will improve our team for our next game. We can control what and how we think, which in turn can impact how we feel. That is immensely powerful.

So, what is our psyche? The psyche is all the thoughts of the human mind, including our conscious and subconscious (unconscious) mind. The subconscious mind records every experience you have ever had and stores this information. It is the seat of all our emotions. The conscious mind, on the other hand, is the mind of reasoning and hence controls the thoughts that are presented from the subconscious. How to control your thoughts is your choice. If the subconscious brings forward a negative thought, your conscious mind can recognize that as true and act on that emotion. On the other hand, you can process the reality of that thought and bring a positive emotion forward instead. Choosing the first can lead to anxiety and false reasoning. As a simple illustration, how many times have you heard a falsehood but believed it to be true? This can lead to stress, negative thoughts, and even wasting time as you try to balance the consequence. However, when one learns that what they heard is not true, or it turns out to be a false rumor, we recognize we wasted precious time with negative thoughts that did not make us feel so good. In turn, these negative emotions affect our personality and how we interact with those around us. Did you ever notice that, when you were around someone in a bad mood or who has a negative attitude, it put you in a bad mood as well? A foul demeanor spills over. The same goes for feeling well when around those in a positive mood; therefore, people like to be around positivity and optimism. Have you ever heard the term positive energy? That is what this is and it is contagious!

It is important to distinguish between intrinsic and extrinsic factors that affect our psyche and recognize what we can manage psychologically. Let me explain. Extrinsic factors are those events happening around us that we have little influence or direct control over. We have control over intrinsic factors and can utilize this to impact our lives and those around us. For example, if someone were to tell you that they do not like your blue shirt, you have two choices: you can become saddened or you can happily confirm that blue is your favorite color and that many others would agree. You have no control over the negative remark, the extrinsic factor, but you have complete control over how that remark makes you feel, the intrinsic factor. We can control our emotions, our feelings, and our overall well-being by managing those intrinsic mental and emotional faculties. While we may be able to influence extrinsic factors in some circumstances, usually we have minimal or no control over the situation that is presented to us. We need to get comfortable with the fact that there is nothing we can do. More importantly, because there is nothing that can be done, we cannot allow it to affect how that makes us feel and act. Seems simple, doesn't it?

Once we have our psyche in check and have gained control of our conscious, subconscious, and how we view and respond to our world around us, it is time to get a better understanding of who we are individually and how we are perceived by those we interact with. That is called emotional intelligence, also termed Emotional Quotient (EQ). Those who understand emotional intelligence and manage it well have a tremendous advantage over those who do not. EQ is not synonymous with Intellectual Quotient (IQ), which is measured by the intelligence tests many of us have taken. Emotional intelligence has become more popular because of its recognized impact on our daily interactions in our everyday roles and on our surroundings. The competencies include two domains: personal and social awareness. Those with a high EQ in personal competence are aware of their emotions and manage their behavior and tendencies. In essence, personal competence is made up of your self-awareness of your emotions and the ability to manage those emotions, behaviors, and tendencies in different situations. Social competence is your ability to understand other people's behaviors, moods, and motives. Having this ability can enhance the quality of relationships and is an essential attribute to success. Imagine if you had high EQ and could develop and manage relationships successfully and how impactful that could be toward achieving your goals. This could enhance happiness for you and those around you. That is a win-win opportunity, wouldn't you say? Self-awareness is a wonderful trait, but even more impactful is learning to modify our behaviors using feedback, which will allow us to be more successful in our human interactions. Please do not confuse this with changing who you are. We are all special in our own ways, and that makes each one of us likable and unique. That diversity of humanity strengthens our individual relationships and social progress.

Communication, and how it is performed, is the final essential characteristic of the attitude principle because human beings have high intellect and sophisticated language abilities. If communication is done correctly and thoughtfully, it can make the difference between success and failure. When we communicate prolifically with positive intonation using affirmative words, the perception and delivery will inspire the receiver. The contrary can deflate or demotivate. I frequently tell people who shy away from difficult discussions that it is not necessarily *what* you say or communicate, it is more often *how* you say it and which words you choose that make the difference in how it is received. This thoughtfulness can result in a reaction that is either confrontational or cooperative. As human beings, we come with different emotional wiring and behaviors, some learned and some inherited. A skilled communicator who understands their personal and social competencies can be a good listener who allows others to share their thoughts fully. That same adroit communicator then effectively brings their point across using language that is not threatening and is received by an audience objectively. This set of skills makes a positive interaction likely, even in the face of delivering difficult news. When it comes to being good at direct, in-person communication, it is often a skill that is innate or learned but can always be refined. Direct communication is an essential tool in perfecting our attitude and delivering our message clearly and positively. Direct communication is both an art and science that, when utilized well, enhances our objectives and success.

Another consideration in reference to communication is the continuous technological change of how we communicate. In this case, the human connection is modified by the involvement of intermediary equipment or software. Texting and e-mail are two examples that are now used to communicate both good and bad news. Because these mediums avoid face-to-face interaction, it is easy to click the send button without thinking of how the communication may be perceived. What we sometimes do not consider is that computers do not have emotions, and the person receiving the message may interpret the message differently than we intended. E-mail and texting etiquette are of utmost importance. It is important to read and reread a message several times before sending it. One must be cognizant of our own mindset and the recipient's emotions when creating a response. Waiting some time to reply to an e-mail and reading a message more than once for the correct interpretation can shed light on an appropriate response. Sometimes on the first read of a message or e-mail, our emotions may influence how we interpret a message. Delaying a response is sometimes of significant benefit. Think about how many times your interpretation of a message has changed as you digest it on a second or third read.

We do not or may not have control over the things that happen around us. We have control over how our own psyche reacts and deals with circumstances. Having a positive outlook, programming our brain to think about things favorably improves our ability to be resilient. A positive attitude will help you achieve your goals and attain success. It brings more happiness into your life; it produces more energy, increases your faith in your abilities, and brings hope for a brighter future. A positive attitude further enables the ability to inspire and motivate yourself and others. You will encounter fewer obstacles and difficulties in your daily life when you are smiling on the inside. You will get more respect from people with a sunny disposition. This phrase may ring like a cliché or a song lyric, but that is because it is so true as to be remarkable: "Smile and the world will smile with you. Frown and frown alone." Remember, you do have control over your attitude, and when you create and project a positive attitude, you are seeding the atmosphere with the very qualities you want reflected back. These qualities support and enhance the effort, values, and results of any team and those surrounding you. It is never too early or too late to train our brain to think in a positive way. The power of our minds is capable of turning lemons into lemonade. It is your choice. That's extraordinary!

Tips

1. Positive words enhance your mood and the attitude of those around you. Use words like *great*, *fantastic*, and *outstanding*. These words affirm inner well-being and get the body's endorphins elevated, which makes you feel good as well as those around you.

2. Greet people when you see and meet them. Always introduce yourself and present your name, smile, make eye contact, and shake the person's hand or offer a fist pump.

3. Learn and use a person's name when you get to know them. People enjoy hearing their own name; it shows you care when you remember, and that has a lasting impact.

4. Listening is as or more important than speaking. Pause in conversation to give a person the opportunity to share their views. People enjoy having an opportunity to be heard.

5. You have control of your psyche. Do not allow your unconscious mind to create circumstances that deflate you. Many things brought forward by your unconscious may not even be true. Utilize your conscious mind to favorably rationalize any situation to keep you in good spirits with positive thoughts.

6. Self-awareness is powerful, but the willingness to adjust as needed is impactful.

7. Carefully select your choice of words in any communication, offering them with a positive intonation. Be careful with using words of blame, such as "you said. . ." Instead, offer a question, such as "didn't you say. . . ?"

8. Stop using negative language in your internal monologue. If something doesn't go as you planned it, don't use phrases like "I messed that up" or "Why can't I do anything right?" Switch your self-examination to a more positive tack by asking yourself, "How can I improve next time?" or "What can I learn from this experience?"

9. Do not let things that are outside of your control bring you down. You might not be able to determine the outcome of a situation, but you can choose how you react to it.

Matters of Fact

- According to the National Center for Education Statistics, direct physical bullying increases in elementary school, peaks in middle school, and declines in high school. A staggering 56 percent of students have personally witnessed some type of bullying at school.[1]
- Attitude can be a factor in many aspects of one's personal health. Researchers from the Maryland School of Medicine found that a good laugh can increase the blood flow throughout your body by 20 percent.[2]

- A review published in the December 2005 issue of *Psychological Bulletin* examined studies of over 275,000 people and found that the happiest people owe their success, in part, to their optimism and positive outlook.[3]
- The following words often attributed to Siddhartha Gautama, philosopher and founder of Buddhism, "All that we are is the result of what we have thought. The mind is everything. What we think we become" capture the essence of the power of our psyche well.[4]
- A study of more than 4,000 people age fifty and older published in the *Journal of Gerontology* demonstrated that having a positive view psychologically enhanced one's belief in their abilities, decreased perceived stress, and fostered healthful behaviors. Physiologically, it lowered c-reactive protein, a marker of stress-related inflammation associated with heart disease and other chronic illnesses, resulting in better health outcomes and enhanced longevity.[5]

PRINCIPLE TWO:
Knowledge and Wisdom
Pursue knowledge; value wisdom.

*"Education is the most powerful weapon
which you can use to change the world."*
Nelson Mandela, 1918–2013,
South African anti-apartheid political leader
and South African president from 1994–1999.

Education is one of the most powerful tools anyone can have. Knowledge is an asset that can never be taken away from you. Facts and skills know no borders and travel with you wherever you go. Information can open doorways of opportunity and insight. Education also offers flexibility. The world changes daily, and to stay current, it is essential to keep learning and reinventing your skill set. Outdated skills become a history lesson in the way it was done. Those dusty skills are possibly no longer of use. That does not mean that all knowledge becomes extinct and has no practical purpose, but in the innovative world we live in, the value of what you know may decline over time as the world advances and changes. The good news is, the access to fresh learnings is readily available to those eager enough to continue to enhance their knowledge base.

The true secret to education is not found within the volume of facts and figures we lock away in our mental libraries. There may be a time when reciting the atomic weight of cesium may come in handy, but it is more likely that you would have the chance to pull out a periodic table and look up cesium's weight should you ever need that number. You would be in trouble if you did not know what the periodic table was or how to read it. The magic of education is that it gives us a framework to engage in creative problem-solving. Education is the mental equivalent of the Boy Scout's ubiquitous motto: "be prepared." No one person can be prepared for every eventuality. What being prepared means is that you are aware of your resources and know how to utilize those assets. Education is the same. While you might not have the answer to a problem in your mind, you have enough knowledge to know how to find the information or resource to solve that quandary.

Whether you have a high school, college, or advanced degree—or no degree at all—it is never too late to start or build upon the foundation you have. Interestingly, the word *commencement* is often used to describe a graduation event.

We tend to think of a graduation ceremony as the end of an educational path; however, the word *commencement* means to start or begin an endeavor. I believe this beginning denotes the educational platform we should continue to build in order to obtain the next stage of learning. That does not necessarily mean that after you graduate from college you should enroll in a master's program. One should aspire to engage in the quest for lifelong learning through formal and informal channels. Formal education, such as taking classes at a university or continuing education classes in your chosen field, allows you to seek additional degrees or certificates of qualification. Informal education can have equal importance. Reading, listening to audiobooks and podcasts, webinars, adult education classes, and going out and trying your hand at a new activity can all contribute to your education. The chances for personal betterment are as limitless as your ambition and imagination.

Formal learning through centers of higher education does have its benefits; however, academic settings can be costly and may not be an avenue of pursuit if one has other obligations. Should formal education be an option, seize the chance and take advantage of the instruction offered. Begin any formal education course or class with your primary goals in mind first. It is fine to take classes based on a passing interest. Your priority, however, should be fulfilling your needs for graduation and your future career versus a fun course your friends are taking. Remember that the primary function of a formal educational setting is to obtain knowledge and a degree or certificate that enhances your value. This will be one of your most important assets as you navigate your future.

Do not fall into the trap of thinking you can learn everything from textbooks. While reading is fundamental in higher educational settings, instructors, professors, and teachers are a wealth of information if you utilize their talents. Gaining from their expertise and presence is one of the reasons formal education is costly. Take advantage of what you are paying for. Your instructors exemplify how theory becomes practice in their given topic or area of expertise. Never be afraid to ask questions or schedule a meeting with an instructor if you need help understanding materials. Most instructors enjoy inquisitive students. Usually, they will offer more of their time knowing you are interested in their expertise and when they can see your passion for learning. Often, an instructor goes into teaching so they can share their knowledge with others who have a passion for their discipline.

If formal education is not an option, informal education can be just as valuable to you. Many employers, especially in creative and tech-based industries, are less interested in degrees and certificates than they are in what you can do. For example, a graphic artist job could hinge on a portfolio's contents rather than a grade point average (GPA). The skills to create that portfolio could have been developed through webinars, podcasts, videos, or other real-world learning experiences. Often these avenues of informal learning can be found free on the internet or be an inexpensive option at venues in your community. There are also free classes and workshops at local stores that can advance your knowledge and skill set. Home Depot and Lowe's, for example, give Do-It-Yourself (DIY) classes on a multitude of marketable skills. Your local library might give you free access to online classes from subscription-based education platforms like Skillshare. Take advantage of these free resources. That's right, they are free! These short seminars can be a wealth of information and offer advanced learning certificates to confirm your participation.

When I was growing up, the *Encyclopedia Britannica* or *World Book Encyclopedia* was the authoritative source for general information. Those tomes would sit on a family's shelves for years, gathering dust and errors. As the world of knowledge moves on, the words in an old encyclopedia become riddled with outdated assumptions and facts. Back then, you had to check the year the encyclopedia was published to ensure you had the latest information. With the internet, outdated information no longer sits on the shelf. Reading articles, journals, and newspapers, or watching YouTube videos, makes information current and accessible. That instant information comes with its own version of checking the encyclopedia's publication date—verification. Any news or educational source on an uncensored internet must be vetted. Does the source come from a peer-reviewed journal or some guy named Bob who is spitballing ideas on a forum? Can you find any credible sources to back up what you are reading? Do the words contain obfuscating language that might hide half-truths?

Verifying sources is especially important in the deluge of social media posts we see daily. Our opinions can be swayed by spurious information. Even truths we hold dear can be shaken when we offhandedly read nonsensical advice from others. During last year's flu season, I saw a post that advocated cutting an onion and putting it by your front door. This practice was common during the Spanish Flu outbreak in 1919 and was thought to trap the germs of anyone who crossed your threshold. That is as ridiculous as stringing garlic up to prevent vampires from coming into your house; however, the person who posted this had a college degree and was married to a PhD. I am sure the repost was due to whimsy and the poster didn't consider the harm that misinformation could cause. Even with those we are familiar with, we should be wary of any media that does not sound quite right.

One method you can use to evaluate information, and many of life's other situations, is to employ critical thinking. There are different models of critical thinking, but this four-step guide will serve you well:

1. Identify your assumptions. (Write your assumptions down for reference and visibility.)
2. Check the accuracy and validity of assertions. (Use credible sources to verify them.)
3. Take alternative perspectives. (Ask yourself: is there more than one answer to consider?)
4. Take informed actions. (Implement the knowledge you have gained.)

Critical thinking is about "self" education as much as it is about following a formula. To identify your assumptions and take alternate perspectives, someone must have a depth of self-awareness that goes beyond the superficial. We must learn and recognize our own limitations and prejudices if we are to evaluate any subjective material or situation. This type of "self" education allows us to synthesize information without personal bias. When we can do that, we have the basis for applying knowledge with wisdom.

My painter friend, Bill, exemplified the importance of the evenhanded application of knowledge by saying, "You need to know more than you need to know." Bill was well studied and enjoyed learning. One day, Bill and his nephew were playing outside. Bill's nephew stepped barefoot into an ant pile and sustained several bites. Bill was not your average painter and had studied chemistry in college. He knew that the ants were in the family *Formicidae* and that the ants' bites contained formic acid. That acid irritates the skin and causes a burning sensation. Bill's analytical chemistry mind kicked into gear, and he soaked his nephew's foot in a baking soda and water bath. After a few minutes of soaking, the pain in his nephew's feet subsided. All Bill had done was apply a basic principle of chemistry. The acidic ants' bites had a low potential for hydrogen (pH) level. Baking soda is a base and has a high pH. Had Bill not had the knowledge to neutralize the acid with a base, he would not have known that this was an option to offer his nephew relief. This was knowledge Bill never thought he would use outside of a chemistry lab. He may never use this nugget of knowledge again, but he used it when it counted.

"Knowing more than you need to know" is a principle that applies to many aspects of life. We should all aspire to continuous learning because we never know when new knowledge or skills will pay off. I intentionally try to learn at least one new thing every day. It may be something I never use, but that is not the point of learning. Education is a joy in and of itself. Obtaining as much knowledge as possible enhances your life and expands your intellect. Knowledge makes you more interesting to the people around you. As your level of knowledge increases, you will have more commonalities to discuss and share with others. Those interactions build and further relationships, which we will talk about in another chapter.

Of all the quotes about the importance and benefits of education and learning, "knowledge is power" frames everything that has been discussed the best. What you do not know, you do not know—no matter how badly you want to know it. From personal experience, I have always been amazed whenever I need to call a maintenance person to fix something at my home. I try to make myself available to watch them make the repair. Often, if the problem is an easy fix, I can do it myself if the problem arises again. This allows me to add to my knowledge base and serves me well. I enjoy taking care of a problem, and I'm saving money on a repair bill as well.

The point about repair work is not solely about being a more enlightened consumer. Having knowledge of repair work gives us the power to make informed decisions. If you understand the repair, the parts, and the time the repairs take, you will have a better idea of whether the costs associated with the repair are reasonable; if you feel comfortable that you can perform it, you have the luxury of deciding if that repair is something you enjoy and want to do or if it would serve you better to have someone else make the repair, giving you the benefit of time to do something else. This level of understanding does not only apply to technical skills. Many intellectual services—such as information technology, how to create basic contracts, or other professional necessities—may be easy to learn or use; however, always be mindful that self-learning has its limitations based on the extent to which you understand the skill or knowledge. It is hubris to think we will never need the guidance or experience of others more skilled or knowledgeable than ourselves.

The limits of education are directly tied to your attitude about learning. Lack of motivation or interest is often the limiting step to education, or anything else for that matter. If you make education fun and challenging for yourself, learning one new thing each day will become an entertaining part of your daily routine. Something you may want to try is, at the end of every day, asking yourself, "What is something new I learned today?" You would be surprised at the new concepts you discover on an average Tuesday. Recapping what you have learned in a day helps to solidify that knowledge in your memory for future use. It may even inspire new thoughts about how something can be done differently, better, or more efficiently. Now that is innovative! If you cannot think of something new you learned on a given day, do a search for a random article on Wikipedia, or research a topic you have heard about but are not too familiar with. The bottom line is that formal and informal education are imperative and must continue if you hope to achieve lifetime success. If a door in life closes, education will open many more.

The only lock that prevents us from opening an educational doorway is fear. We have established that, via the internet, information on any topic is readily available. So why would anyone fear learning something new? The fear is not of learning itself but of failing to learn or the need to change. *What if I cannot comprehend the information? What if I find out I am not as smart as I once thought I was? What if something I knew is now outdated or no longer preferred?* The litany of fear-based reactions to learning is as infinite as the reasons not to do anything new. The truth is that our reality is one of constant motion. We are intellectual sharks that swim the seas of information. If we stop swimming, we will be swallowed by the change of a new day.

With the world changing so quickly, obtaining knowledge of as many things as possible will only position you to lead and be successful in the future. We can look no further than some well-known companies to validate this assertion. For example, we know the company Nokia as a telecommunication firm, but the corporation was originally founded in 1865 as a paper mill. The Nintendo company started out producing playing cards in 1902. Have you ever rented a movie from Blockbuster, created a MySpace page, or sent a text on a Blackberry? Do not worry if you haven't; you are in the majority. These companies could not, or did not, adapt to their marketplaces and paid a hefty price.

The companies that fail forget that being an industry leader means having a vision past their moment in the sun.

Individual mastery of a certain discipline is not limited to gaining immediate knowledge but also extends to how to apply that knowledge to the future. There are businesses that have been built on being the subject expert and offering consultative services to advise on future concerns. Many industries are impacted by regulations and other requirements that are not part of their core line of business. Consulting services also exist because there is simply too much information for one person, or a group of people, to know; therefore, businesses may need a subject expert to offer opinions on compliance in their industry. The power of subject knowledge offers additional opportunities beyond the knowledge itself for a person interested and eager enough to spend the time to gain it. Did you know that Thomas Jefferson never went to law school but passed the bar? In the state of Virginia, you can sit for the bar exam with an approved apprenticeship rather than a law degree. If you pass the test, you are a lawyer.

Read fervently and be creative and innovative, which will position you for success. In school, creativity is not graded or judged; however, creativity has sparked many of our greatest inventions. Also, know that the road to creativity and success is not always easy or well defined. Using the touchstone of American innovation, Thomas Edison, a bellwether for creativity, found dozens of apocryphal stories. Edison supposedly did not speak until he was age four. In his attempt to create the light bulb, he failed thousands of times. It's not what Thomas Edison did that we should focus on here but the four tenets taught to Edison by his mother. Those principles were:

1. Never get discouraged if you fail. Learn from it. Keep trying.
2. Learn with both your head and hands.
3. Not everything of value in life comes from books—experience the world.
4. Never stop learning. Read the entire panorama of literature.

The providence of these items does not matter because the advice is sound. Jane Smith's mom from Anytown, USA could have said these four principles and they would be just as true. Creative thinking like this has allowed me to develop several instruments that have improved surgical practice. I have edited a medical text and acted as a consultant to several companies on various innovative topics. I am an invited lecturer on subjects related to clinical medicine, medical management, and leadership. In addition, I have authored or coauthored numerous peer-reviewed and invited publications that have shared my learnings and experiences. I have contributed toward better child health outcomes and enhanced opportunities for all generations through my passion for the betterment of humankind. I wish the same for you. I encourage you to latch onto a subject you are so passionate about that you cannot wait to learn about it every day and share your knowledge and wisdom with others. Those who can do that have truly found their calling. That's extraordinary!

Tips

1. Explore opportunities in your current job to continue your education. Many employers offer free or reduced-price access to online learning environments like Skillshare or offer reimbursements for college classes. Employers often offer these as perks. Taking advantage of these free or reduced-cost educational opportunities could help you transition into your next job.

2. If you cannot imagine what the world or job market might be in the next ten years, seek out articles and books from futurists. These people make predictions about the future based on socioeconomic and political trends.

3. Recognizing the style of learning that is best suited to you will not only make learning more fun but will also set you up for successfully absorbing new knowledge. Pinpoint whether a visual, auditory, or hands-on learning style resonates with you.

4. Informal or nontraditional education is not about being valedictorian. Understand that your only competition is with yourself and the goal is to grasp the concepts to enhance your knowledge.

5. A time-honored German adage says, "You will become clever through your mistakes." We grow through resistance and missteps, so embrace the things that move you to greater heights.

Matters of Fact

- Creativity and need are the mother of invention. Did you know that research shows that only 2 percent of forty-four-year-olds are creative? In contrast, 98 percent of four-year-olds are considered creative.[6]

- The median number of years that wage and salary job-holders work for a single employer is only 4.2 years, according to an economic news release from the Bureau of Labor Statistics. This longevity varies by the age of the employee and their occupation.[7]

- It is estimated that the average person will change careers twelve times during their working life, according to career change statistics.[8]

- Creativity has benefits to your everyday life, including as a means for stress relief and problem-solving and as an outlet for expression.[9]

- In 1999, the age-adjusted mortality rate of high school dropouts ages twenty-five to sixty-four was more than twice as large as the mortality rate of those with some college. Staying in school will not only benefit you financially but will give you a longer life span.[10]

- Accepted facts change: two dozen modern studies have revealed that the average human body temperature isn't 98.6°F and that the new average is closer to 97.5°F. There's always a need to refresh what we believe to be immutable truths.[11]

- In 1962, E. M. Rogers developed the Diffusion of Innovation Theory, which expresses five distinct types of people who latch onto new technologies, ideas, or social mores. Rogers's theory is used in business schools today to illustrate the point. The five types are Innovators (2.5 percent), Early Adopters (13.5 percent), Early Majority (34 percent), Late Majority (34 percent), and Laggards (16 percent). The five groups form a bell curve. There's not a lot of company when charting untested waters, so don't worry about being alone when trying new things. The rest of the world will catch up![12]

- In 2017, 5.4 percent of high school students dropped out of school.[13] Furthermore, 56 percent of college students who started a four-year degree dropped out of classes.[14] Among first-time college students who enrolled in a four-year degree, only 41 percent graduated on time. Of those who did graduate, 59 percent earned their bachelor's degree in six years.[15]

Relationships and Community

Nurture interpersonal bonds.

*"Personal relationships are the fertile soil
from which all advancement, all success,
all achievement in real life grows."*
Ben Stein, b. 1944, American writer, lawyer, actor,
comedian, and political and economic commentator.

A few years ago, the game show *Who Wants to Be a Millionaire?* topped TV ratings. A single contestant is asked increasingly difficult multiple-choice questions. Each correct answer is rewarded with an ever-increasing cash prize. If the contestant gets all the questions correct, the reward is a cool million dollars. The show differentiates itself from other quiz shows by allowing the contestant a little help called lifelines. If a question is too difficult, the contestant can call a friend or expert for advice, ask the audience's opinion on the right answer, or reduce the choices to a 50 percent chance of picking the correct answer. One might think that asking an expert would lock in going home a million dollars richer. Chances are, if you make that phone call, you'll go home with parting gifts.

The journalist James Surowiecki studied large, complex groups versus individuals or small group decision-making in situations like *Who Wants to Be a Millionaire?* in an article for the *New Yorker* titled "The Wisdom of Crowds." His research found that calling for outside help got contestants the correct answer 61 percent of the time. Asking the audience gave an astonishing correct answer rate of 91 percent. Groups exhibiting a synergy of intellect were not unique to the audience of *Who Wants to Be a Millionaire?* Surowiecki discovered that large groups of people are smarter together than a select few—no matter how intelligent those few are individually. His research found that large groups innovate quicker, make better decisions collectively, and forecast future events better than individuals.[16]

How can Surowiecki be correct? We are taught that iconoclastic innovators are of equal symbolic importance to Americans as apple pie. That is because we have been taught to focus on leaders. Even the guidelines that brought Thomas Edison success were not his rules. Those maxims were supposedly taught to Edison by his mother. Edison's Menlo Park was an intellectual factory that churned out the technology our present-day world is built upon; however, Edison did not spend his days and nights alone tinkering with inventions. At its height, Menlo Park employed fifty to sixty skilled tradesmen, PhDs, chemists, and engineers.[17] Edison's example shows that no matter how brilliant you may be alone, amazing things can be achieved when you surround yourself with quality people.

The entire concept of relationships and building community revolves around creating dynamic and genuine connections between yourself and others. I have always valued my relationships. I love people, and the more people I can get to know and learn from, the happier and better person I become. Relationships come in many forms—family, friends, business associates, or acquaintances you strike up a conversation with at a social gathering or in line for a movie. No matter what the relationship is, always be thankful for that person. Never take any relationships for granted, and always give more of yourself than you expect ever to get back. Most importantly, enter a relationship because you want to, not because you must.

The most important relationship you will ever enter will be between yourself and your spouse or life partner. I believe the person you decide to spend your life with will be the single most important decision you will ever make. This person will be there to see you at your greatest and most vulnerable moments. Your partner will be with you for every major life decision. As you advance in your career, your spouse or significant other will have a hand in your development. Every facet of your life will be affected by your chosen person. Even though that relationship begins at home, it extends far beyond the borders of your living space.

With everything that has been said about this person's importance in your life, that statement sounds obvious, but it is not. You can love someone and still decide they are not the right person to enter a lifetime partnership with. Matters of the heart can cloud one's judgment. Often, we overlook red flags in someone we have romantic feelings for because "they're a good person" or "it will get better when we're together all of the time." There will be a temptation to enter a long-term relationship when the timing in your life is wrong because you are afraid of losing that person, who might just be filling a particular void at that time in your life. If you are in a relationship and there are any aspects of it that do not resonate with your goals or present situation, you would be prudent to reevaluate the relationship and its long-term viability. If you do not believe the importance of this spousal relationship to be true, just ask someone who has had the unfortunate experience of a divorce or life-partner separation and learn from their experience.

If the time and place in your life are right for partnering up with someone, examine why you want to spend the rest of your life with this person. Physical attraction, shared history, or similar tastes are factors that should be present in any union. Many people would say that having the same views on religion and politics are key factors to a happy partnership. I would argue that differences in ideologies can sometimes be overcome. Focus on commonalities where it comes to a shared sense of purpose. Those strengths—with emphasis on that importance, along with mutual compromise—will allow for a successful relationship. If you are with someone who shares your "big goal," everything else is in the details. Not talking about sports or politics at the dinner table or buying crunchy as opposed to smooth peanut butter all pale in comparison to not having the same goals. Find a partner who wants the same broad things in life that you do. If you want to be a travel photographer and see the world and your potential partner's goal is to raise a family, these goals would nearly be impossible to achieve together. When you find that the person and the timing are right, it will happen. Finding your person might take longer than you anticipated, but it is worth the wait. Then show your partner you are grateful for your relationship every day. Focus on the big picture and do not sweat the small stuff.

I got married a little later in life. I wanted to complete my surgical training before sharing my life with someone else. I was committed to being a child advocate and developing my skills as a pediatric surgical subspecialist. I had discussed this choice with the director of the fellowship program I trained with in Virginia. He knew how devoted I was to my profession and poked fun at me about my dedication. He often told me that I would never get married because medicine was my calling and the love of my life. All that changed when I moved to Miami and met my beautiful wife, Patricia. She is everything I could have imagined I wanted in a life partner. I also met her at a time in my life when I could devote the necessary energy to building a home with someone else. Patricia is my best friend and the mother of my two beautiful children.

Relationships require diligence and work if you want to maintain them. A good life partnership, or any other relationship, is built upon synergy where all parties benefit from each other's success. It will require compromise and not always getting what you want for yourself. This comes from recognizing that there are no individual winners in a relationship. Each party's achievements should be equally shared and celebrated. You did not get that promotion at work alone. A good partner would have been there as your lifeline through the late nights and work-at-home sessions. That goes for associates, colleagues, and others as they support your success and you support theirs. It's the relationships with people you get to know and count on that elevate you and make life easier, even during tough times. This begins with the support of a life partner.

You will find that while waltzing through life with your partner, your lives will invariably intersect with the lives of others. The more lives you touch, the more you will learn about and understand the people around you—and the more knowledge you gain and the more opportunity it will create. You and your partner will create your own community based on these interactions. We tend to think of communities as larger and grander than a circle of friends or a select group of professionals who get together for coffee once a month. For our purposes, a community is a group of any size that is bound together by a commonality. Humans, and most living beings, are hardwired to form communities. The need to form groups is a biological imperative that increases the chances of survival. The most basic level of community is, of course, one's family. Children are bound to, and dependent on, their parents for survival during their youth and then care for their parents in their elder years. This cycle creates a natural order and desire to be part of a group. That yearning to be a part of something bigger than oneself does not go away as we get older. We find that, in groups, we can create and achieve more than we ever could on our own.

Understanding the power of creating individual communities and connections is imperative to living an extraordinary life. It is easy to overlook how communities work on a micro level when we see the impact of larger community efforts. For example, after a natural disaster, people band together to ease the suffering of their neighbors. Always holding ourselves and the communities we are part of up to always performing world-changing actions is unrealistic. Surrounding yourself with people who wish to make a positive impact on others is what day-to-day community-building is about. The simple act of giving someone a ride when their car is in the shop or calling someone to check on them is how individual communities are built. You never know how those small acts of mutual aid and support may impact someone or how developing a community can aid you. As you continue to help others, you may not even realize how that connection has been paid forward to someone else or returned to you for something you may need. That is the power of relationships. You may be exceptionally qualified or have certain skill sets that, if someone you know is aware of them because of your relationship, may open doors and produce opportunities not readily available had the connection not been established.

The old saying "It's not what you know, it's who you know" is only half true. No number of personal connections will cover a lack of talent or ability. Conversely, showing exceptional skill and aptitude can attract an opportunity. Those who have seen the musical *Hamilton*, or are history buffs, will recognize both elements in the relationship between George Washington and Alexander Hamilton. It was Hamilton's bravery amidst the calamitous New York campaign of 1776 and the tide-turning battles of Trenton and Princeton in 1777 that caught Washington's attention. Hamilton would become Washington's aide-de-camp for much of the Revolutionary War. Washington and Hamilton were nowhere close to being friends. Their relationship was always on a professional footing. It was Hamilton's ability to proficiently execute his duties that kept him in Washington's orbit—not any personal kinship the two had. Hamilton was selected to be the first secretary of the Treasury Department after the conclusion of the Revolutionary War. In that post, Alexander Hamilton created the financial system that fuels our government to this day.[18] The relationship between Hamilton and Washington illustrates how community and connections create mutually beneficial opportunities.

Another element of the Washington and Hamilton relationship that is not often explored is the gratitude Hamilton felt toward Washington. Interspersed in Hamilton's letters are recognitions of Washington's contribution to Hamilton's life. We will discuss "an attitude of gratitude" in another section of this book by showing the importance of appreciating the people in our communities. We show our gratitude to those who give, open a door, or mentor us by excelling at the opportunities given to us and by giving others breaks into areas they may not be fortunate enough to access alone. Years ago, I met an undergraduate student from my alma mater who was interested in medical school. I spoke with him about what to expect and how to prepare for the life of a doctor. We have kept in touch through the years, and I have enjoyed watching him grow into an accomplished physician. He frequently expresses his thanks for the short conversations we have and the advice or direction I have offered. I am often amazed at the impact that some intermittent conversations, a small amount of time spent sharing some life experiences and suggestions, could have on someone else's path. Just as enjoyable is the satisfaction I receive from being able to help someone else in their career aspirations and how much I have learned from the experience. I am grateful for that.

The truth is, we never fully know how far the impact of our tiny communities can reach. Mathematician and meteorologist Edward Lorenz developed a metaphorical example of chaos theory known as the "butterfly effect." The theory is that small changes in a system, like a butterfly flapping its wings halfway around the world, can be the start of larger consequences, like the formation of a tornado. If we were to apply the butterfly effect theory to our positive actions within our communities, we could never track the cascading effects of kindness and gratitude. That makes it anyone's best practice to form genuine, vulnerable, and honest connections with everyone you meet.

Making positive connections is especially important in the information age. Social media interactions help fill the previously discussed biological imperative for group-building and bridging the gap between the cyberworld and real life. We can look to the origins of Meetup as an example of cyberspace at its best. The website was created in 2002 by Scott Heiferman and five others to bring together people of similar hobbies and interests. Heiferman lived in New York City at the turn of the last century and had never met any of his neighbors, but the September 11, 2001, attacks on the World Trade Center and the Pentagon became Scott's impetus to reach out to those who lived around him. The deterioration of community in America had made any story of neighborhoods coming together to meet their neighbors' needs as newsworthy as the September 11 attacks. Scott Heiferman decided to do something about that. The next year, Meetup was born with the avowed purpose of bringing people together. Meetup was launched a year before MySpace and two years before Facebook. One could argue that Meetup was one of the internet's first social networks and influenced how society interacts today.

You can make use of social networks in a positive manner, just like the founders of Meetup did. Never in human history have we been able to communicate so easily and freely with those in our community. You should be mindful of the content and comments you post. The butterfly effect of social networking can work positively and negatively. It is also difficult to gauge subtleties in a short post. Take the time to consider how your words will affect anyone who reads them. (Don't be the person who advises putting a cut-up onion at your front door to keep the flu away.) You can never go wrong with being silent if you are not sure you're making a positive impact with your words. Emotions feed on emotions, so the more good thoughts you put out, the more good energy you will receive.

On any level of community or connection, from life partner to newfound friend, the goal is to create an open dialogue in which everyone benefits. When we are genuinely interested and invested in those around us, they will return that interest. At times it can be difficult to open yourself up and share with others. These are the times when you receive the greatest rewards. Author Brené Brown describes facing these situations "with strong backs, soft fronts, and wild hearts." If we can open ourselves to creating connections and a community with those three things, there is nothing we can't do and achieve. That's extraordinary!

Tips

1. Send a "nice to meet you" message after exchanging e-mail addresses, social media information, or business cards with a new contact. This helps solidify the connection, and people will remember you when you do so.

2. Get to know people and spend more time listening and learning about others' interests, families, and accolades. Getting to know people and learning about them, and having them learn about you, has mutual benefits.

3. Find the things you have in common with others around you. This may be a shared favorite sports team or movie, an activity you both enjoy, or maybe just where you are from. This helps to forge a connection when building relationships. People choose friends by commonalities.

4. Remember, relationships are built on trust, honesty, and respect. Establishing these core principles in a relationship enables many mutual benefits and opportunities.

5. Allow for a balanced interaction. Being a skilled communicator allows one to build relationships and encourage others to help you grow and succeed.

6. Always have physical or virtual business cards at the ready. You never know when you will meet someone you want to remain in contact with. Hand out your cards liberally.

7. Become part of community groups on social networking sites to keep abreast of neighborhood news, occasions to be of service, and opportunities to expand your personal and professional network.

Matters of Fact

- Loneliness and feelings of isolation can be as bad for someone's health as having a long-term illness such as diabetes or high blood pressure.[19]
- Friendships are among the most essential and supportive types of relationships you will ever establish because while family relationships are (typically) nonnegotiable, friendship is a voluntary institution.[20]
- A ten-year study by the Center of Ageing at Flinders University found that a strong network of friends improves one's odds of beating serious illnesses and can even extend one's life-span.[21]
- A 2015 Harvard University Business School study showed that hiring one highly toxic employee can be more harmful to the bottom line than several cooperative yet less productive employees. Being a good member of your community matters.[22]
- Four things American psychological researcher and clinician Professor John Gottman says couples should never do are:

  1. Criticize each other
  2. Show contempt

3. Be defensive
4. Stonewall discussions about problems

Gottman should know. He did extensive work over a four-decade career studying divorce prediction and marital stability. The same should hold true for any personal or professional relationship you find yourself in.[23]

- Professor Garth Fletcher, in his book *The Science of Intimate Relationships*, claims that "women are more expert and motivated relationship managers than men." The men in the audience should take note and seek counsel from their female counterparts if they feel they are lacking in the relationship-building arena.[24]

- A United Kingdom employee engagement firm, Wildgoose, polled employees from 120 diverse businesses. When rating workplace satisfaction, they found that 61 percent of those surveyed felt positive workplace relationships meant as much or more than salary.[25]

- The average person forms 396 personal relationships over their lifetime. Of those, about one-third will be considered close friends, while the rest can be labeled as social friendships.[26]

PRINCIPLE FOUR:
Sustainable Wealth
Manage income to achieve wealth.

*"The habit of saving is itself an education; it fosters
every virtue, teaches self-denial, cultivates the sense of
order, trains to forethought, and so broadens the mind."*
T. T. Munger, 1883–1975, groundbreaking research
scientist for the United States Forest Service
who founded the Wind River Experimental Forest.

Money is a topic like math. Some instinctively understand the overarching concepts behind the language of
the universe, then there are those of us who struggled
with the problems and had to get extra tutoring. In that
respect, the biggest difference between math and money is
that personal finance classes are not part of many graduation
requirements. Without any outside guidance, many adults

are ill prepared to effectively manage their money, which can be one of life's greatest stressors; however, if you come up with a financial plan and a budget, stick to them, and keep your financial health in check, it will alleviate much of that stress in your life.

I was forced to learn how to budget early in life. Coming from a modest middle-class family with several siblings, I knew I was more fortunate than many. Still, there were limitations to what my parents could offer and afford. I often held odd jobs throughout school and during the summer months to help pay for my expenses, but I will never forget my first real paycheck from my first full-time job. At the time, I was living in Manhattan as a surgical intern. It was the first paycheck of my medical career and was for a whopping $600. I did not know if I should frame the check or cash it. I ended up cashing it because I needed the money. Six hundred dollars every two weeks did not seem like it would stretch far in Manhattan—and it didn't. I had to account for every penny to make it work for me in the Big Apple.

The lessons from living lean have always stuck with me and formed my own money learning laboratory. Through the lens of time, I have seen how those lessons have turned into a universal financial plan. Like most complex subjects, money matters can be broken down into simpler components. Income, expenses, and savings are the three pillars of any financial plan. If you can understand each, you will be well on your way to understanding personal finances. I often think of it as a three-legged stool. If one of the three legs is not in balance, then the stool is likely to fall over. On the most basic level, one's income must be higher than one's expenses. Any excess income should go into savings. Achieving a positive cash flow takes budgeting, making good decisions, having discipline, and creating a solid financial plan. Before charting out a financial course, understand that budgets and planning are tools for success. To gain full control of your financial future, keep in mind that all money matters are about the relationship between you and your money.

Money is more than a medium of exchange between two entities. Money is a contract that says, "I give you my best effort for the finest good or services you can provide." When financial matters are viewed in this context, money becomes a function of time, expertise, and work ethic. If we extend the metaphor, a budget for one's income and expenses turns into an exercise on how you expend effort during your workday. To bring this point home, let us say you are shopping for a new car. You have done your due diligence and estimated your monthly loan payment for your dream car. The monthly payment fits your budget, and you are almost set to buy it. Before you head to the dealership, you run one more calculation on the car's cost. With the principal and interest of your car loan, that car will cost you six months' salary. When viewed in terms of half a year's work, is that car really worth it now? Although many people think of a car as an investment, it loses value the minute you drive it off the lot; therefore, it is not an investment at all. In the face of a financial emergency, selling the vehicle will never get you back your initial spend. The age of the vehicle, number of miles on it, and the overall condition further decrease the car's value; therefore, you must consider your financial status to determine if you need a car for transportation or if it's a luxury item that your budget can afford. This is a good lesson in the importance of discipline and budgeting for a long-term plan opposed to the immediate pleasure of personal gratification.

There is also often a mental disconnect between one's career and the income that a career generates. If this were not the case, everyone on a stellar career path would also be on easy street financially speaking. We know through personal anecdotal examples this is not always the case. Every day, some are at the pinnacle of their careers and yet surprisingly file for bankruptcy. In these cases, I would bet you could ask the career-savvy person, "Where do you see your career in five years?" and receive a flawless answer. Of equal importance is a question each of these people could not answer, "Where do you see your finances in five years?" Marrying the planning and execution skills we use every day in our professions with a mindset of spending one's effort (in the form of money) will create an extraordinary financial future for you, no matter your income level. Were he still alive, this is something you would not need to tell George Clason, author of the quick read *The Richest Man in Babylon*. Clason offered expert wisdom with seven simple rules that any disciplined person can follow for a more secure financial future.

1. Start thy purse to fattening: save money.
2. Control thy expenditures: don't spend more than you need.
3. Make thy gold multiply: invest wisely.

4. Guard thy treasures from loss: avoid investments that sound too good to be true.
5. Make of thy dwelling a profitable investment: own your home.
6. Ensure a future income: protect yourself with life insurance.
7. Improve thy ability to earn: strive to become wiser and more knowledgeable.[27]

Those concepts seem easy but are not practiced by most people.

Do you remember being asked as a kid, "What do you want to be when you grow up?" You must ask yourself a similar question about your finances. What do you want your life to look like? These are the starting points of financial planning. You do not have to use spreadsheets or find an accountant to chart your overall goals. You first must understand where you are currently, where you want to go, and where you want to end up. Again, this sounds like a basic concept, but it is often forgotten in the trenches of life. We work to shape the life and future we want.

An extraordinary life is lived when there is homeostasis between one's income and lifestyle. If you wish to lead an extravagant lifestyle, then do so if you have the income to support it. In that situation, one's income and lifestyle are in balance. It is when we do not achieve balance that money problems crop up. Living a lifestyle that exceeds your income can create high-interest debt. There has never been a debt taken out that was not stressful to repay. The flip side of extravagance is living so frugally there is nothing in your life that brings you joy. If you can afford to go on a vacation but do not because you must save money no matter the impact on your well-being, that is a problem. How can we succeed in our careers and be of service to others if we are so cost conscious we cannot enjoy our own existence? Like Goldilocks, you must find the balance between income and lifestyle that is just right for you.

Again, financial balance starts with living within your means. At any point in your life, you may be tempted to match your lifestyle with your peers'. If Larry from accounting was able to afford an inground swimming pool, then so should I! A keeping-up-with-the-Joneses mentality will only succeed in increasing your debt and chasing someone else's dream. Living an extraordinary life is not about keeping a lifestyle that is centered around impressing your peers. An extraordinary life comes from having a sustainable lifestyle that brings you joy and security. Most people know the story about the tortoise and the hare. The hare ran the race so fast at the beginning that he was exhausted and never made it to the finish line; however, the tortoise was slow, but steady, throughout the race and won. Coming up with a financial plan and budget that considers the plan's value over time and using the three buckets discussed above of income, expenses, and savings is simple and an easy methodology to work with. A sustainable plan takes into account two components of life, that is, your needs and wants. First, there are those items that we need to live, such as food, shelter, clothing, and other essential necessities. There is no mistake when we call these

"NEEDS," so they are budgeted for from the beginning. Second, there are those items that we want for our enjoyment. These are our "WANTS," so we can do with or without them, more or less depending on our financial circumstances. To go back to our car analogy, you may need a car to get to work, but it can be a used Toyota or a new Porsche. The "NEED" is the transportation to get to work as public transportation may not be readily available where you live. The "WANT" is a new car versus a used one and a Porsche versus a Toyota.

There may also be the potential for a compromise if you can afford a new Toyota. It would offer both the necessary transportation and the enjoyment of the new vehicle you long for without the cost of the luxury sports car price tag. This is the area where discipline and reason come into play. Sacrificing the "WANT," or part of it, allows for needs to be filled and security to be obtained. Personally, I drive a twenty-year-old Toyota 4Runner. When I purchased the car, I bought it new off the lot at the end of the year as that gave me the best value for my money and offered me the new car I had been hoping for. Twenty years later, I still enjoy the truck, and it remains reliable. Best of all, my 4Runner has no car payment. That was a good choice for me.

Many books teach the concept "pay yourself first," which means 10 percent of your monthly paycheck should be put into a retirement account or fund. This is the savings part of the equation. The remainder of the money can then be allocated to the other budget buckets. Not everyone can do this at first, but even if you can commit a small amount early on, it gets you into a savings habit. Besides, when you see your savings grow over time, wow, does that make you smile and feel secure. I cannot stress enough that the tool that brings your financial balance in focus is a budget. You do not have to dream up a budget all on your own. There are financial resources on the web, or your local bank may offer financial counselors if you need a little tutoring. I found a sample budget on the web that gives a good approximation of how your total income could be allocated.

> Giving: 10–15 percent
> Medical: 5–10 percent
> Housing: 25–35 percent
> Transportation: 10–15 percent
> Savings: 10–15 percent
> Food: 10–15 percent
> Utilities: 5–10 percent
> Insurance: 10–20 percent
> Recreation: 5–10 percent
> Clothing: 2–5 percent
> Personal: 5–10 percent[28]

This is by no means the perfect budgetary framework for every situation. You will have to adjust based on your individual needs and circumstances, but the example is a good ruler with a range of how much of your income should be spent in which areas. Remember, the total percentage should equal no more than 100 percent; otherwise, your income and expenses are out of balance. In this situation, you may have to borrow money to cover your expenses. This course may be necessary, but one must be thoughtful if they do take on debt as it will mean taking on an added interest expense to pay it back. The goal is not to have debt if you can help it. My father always shared that the only debt you should take on is a home mortgage. A home is likely the one necessary expenditure you will not be able to fully pay cash for because of the expense. When considering how much a person can afford to spend on a home, there is a general rule that a home 2–2.5 times the value of your annual income is within your means. If you make an annual salary of $50,000, you should be able to afford a home that costs in the $100,000–125,000 range. What people forget to include when budgeting for a home is the expense for running it—the cost of utilities, maintenance, annual property taxes, and an emergency fund for any unknowns. An additional thought is that most people do not want to be what you call "house poor." That means you have nothing left over for enjoyment and savings because everything you spend is going toward the house. This can quickly become disheartening.

Be cautious of the 2–2.5 times rule that many realtors or mortgage bankers may share. Aside from the nicety of owning a home, the other benefit of home ownership is that a house is generally considered an investment as it usually increases in value over time; however, you must realize that is not a definitive statement. Housing markets and the condition of a home at the time you need or want to sell will affect the house's price. Also, there are costs to buying and selling a home called closing costs. When deciding to buy a home, consider those items and sit down with someone educated on this topic to assist you in understanding what you can really afford and what you are agreeing to. The saddening financial crisis of 2008 left many people unable to pay their mortgages and their homes foreclosed on by the banks as variable interest rate loans made monthly payments impossible for some. We can often get emotionally excited about something because of its beauty and our desires without considering the possible longer-term consequences of the decision if things do not go as planned.

Here is another concept to keep in mind when thinking about your budget or anything you spend. This is called the Return on Investment (ROI). In the business world, ROI is the ratio between an item of expenditure and the profit received by that expense. For example, if you owned a delivery company and purchased a van for $30,000, you would expect that van to generate at least $30,001 to have a return on your investment. Using the principle of ROI works in your personal life too. If you cannot find the ROI in purchasing something, maybe you should reevaluate that expense. In personal finances, not everything you invest in will bring you a cash return; however, you should expect to get a certain amount of utility for your investment. Before you spend money on a good or service, you should evaluate that good's or service's ROI. Ask yourself a few simple questions:

- Will buying this fit my budget?
- What benefit will I derive from this?
- Can I live without it or find an alternative?
- Am I receiving value for my money?

The goal of this exercise staves off the unpleasantness of buyer's remorse. Few feelings are akin to realizing you have traded your best effort for something that doesn't fit your needs. When you apply these questions to every purchase you make, you will save yourself money. Most of the money we waste is not on big purchases. Most people spend time examining big-ticket item purchases, but we forget the impact small purchases have on our finances.

Multimillionaire real estate tycoon Tim Gurner started a discussion about the effects of discretionary spending during a 2017 *60 Minutes* interview. Gurner memorably said, "When I was trying to buy my first home, I wasn't buying smashed avocado [on toast] for nineteen dollars and four coffees at four dollars each."[29] Tim's point is that little expenses add up over time. Not reining in wasteful spending habits, even if they are inside your budget, can make you miss out on your larger financial goals. Every dollar we needlessly expend makes our long-term goals more difficult to reach. I share with my children the analogy that every dollar they earn is a soldier. They need to send their soldiers out to fight for them and capture other soldiers, growing their savings account with interest or other financial growth opportunities. Every soldier that they spend is a soldier that was captured by the other side. It is necessary to spend soldiers as part of life, but this should be done thoughtfully, strategically, and with discipline. One can use this concept even in retirement: the more soldiers guarding their castle, the easier one's golden years will be. The nice thing is the soldiers (dollars) never die in my analogy. They just move from one place to another.

That shuffling of troops enables us to enjoy our lives and our personal economies to succeed.

To further emphasize the point, balancing financial priorities is a behavior exhibited regardless of personal wealth. There are those among the ultra-rich who understand expense management and embrace cost-saving measures in their personal lives. Most famously, Warren Buffett, CEO of Berkshire Hathaway, has a net worth of $88.9 billion. He still lives in the same five-bedroom, two-and-a-half-bath house he bought in 1958. David Cheriton, a Stanford professor, whose $100,000 investment in Google netted him a cool $1 billion, still drives a 1986 Volkswagen and cuts his own hair. Thomas J. Stanley, the author of *Stop Acting Rich* and *The Millionaire Next Door*, claimed in a 2010 blog post that the median price of motor vehicles purchased by millionaires was $31,367.[30] A fully loaded Honda Accord would have been the perfect new car for a millionaire.

The obvious takeaway from rich people saving money is that cutting expenses allows you to save more of your income. That income can be invested; therefore, one can more easily build their individual financial empire toward financial freedom. It is all about keeping as many soldiers as you can. While that logic is sound, the real message from the previous examples is found in "why." Warren Buffett, when asked about his house, says he would move if he thought he would be happier. David Cheriton obviously has a sentimental connection to his old Volkswagen that makes buying a newer car unthinkable. Stanley's unnamed millionaires understand that a car is a tool to get from one place to another. "Getting there in style" isn't worth the $650 oil changes that come with the flash of driving a Rolls-Royce or Bentley. The relationship between these people and their money is that money is an instrument for the security to pursue happiness.

One of the greatest threats to financial security and balance is unchecked debt. A good rule of thumb is to only go into debt if there is an emergency or if the debt will give you a positive ROI. For example, taking out student loans to complete college is an investment in your future earnings. Someone with a bachelor's degree is estimated to earn 66 percent more over a forty-year career than a person with a high school diploma.[31] With that ROI, student loans make sense. As shared above, home mortgages are another example of a good ROI on taking out debt. In general, homes appreciate at a rate of 3–5 percent a year. Also, a home provides shelter, one of our basic essential needs.

What is not a wise use of debt is buying things you do not absolutely need with credit cards. According to the Federal Reserve, the average annual interest rate for credit cards as of the first quarter of 2019 was 15.09 percent.[32] If you charge $1,000 on that average rate credit card and pay it off over the year, you will incur $83 in interest charges. Many chains and online stores also offer lines of credit with worse terms. Amazon offers a store card with a 27.74 percent interest rate. Amazon offers some no-interest promotion options for balances paid off within six or twelve months.[33] But at the end of the promotion period, you are stuck with paying the exorbitant interest rate. In real terms, if you purchase $1,000 worth of items using Amazon's credit card, you will owe $156 in interest.

Financial planning, budgeting, watching discretionary spending, and meaningful use of debt—why does any of this matter? There will always be more money to make. There will always be a side hustle out there to help make ends meet. Won't there? We work hard to create a life we enjoy and to plan for the inevitable. Your car will break down on the way to an important meeting. A storm will knock out the electricity right after you have done all your shopping for Thanksgiving dinner. Hosts of other problems will crop up that will require you to spend outside of your budget. No matter what your take on the Bible is, the writer of Ecclesiastes understood the role of money in adulting:

> "A feast is made for laughter, and wine makes merry,
> but money answers everything." Ecclesiastes 10:19

To understand this quote, know it was not meant to be literal. We read it in the context of Solomon speaking to God and promoting the philosophy that the best life is having enough to eat and drink and enjoying the work it takes to earn it. Every time one of these inevitable situations comes up and you are caught short on money, you'll wish that you had had the discipline to cut back on your spending. Purchasing four cups of coffee and avocado toast every day will seem foolish when your budgeted emergency fund is not enough to bail you out of a pickle.

The biggest inevitability, and possibly the hardest to emotionally process, is that one day we will all retire from our careers. The steps you take now in savings and investing will have a huge impact on what your life will look like when you transition into a life of leisure. Think about this—if you invested $1,000 a year in the stock market for the next twenty years at the average return rate of 8 percent, you would net $45,762. Every investment carries a certain amount of risk, and your returns can never be guaranteed. However, the $1,000-a-year example illustrates the power of saving over time. Take advantage of every savings opportunity you can afford. Some employers offer matching 401(k) programs that will help with growing your savings. If they offer matching contributions, they are offering free money to incentivize you to put money away. It makes no sense to turn away additional pay in the form of retirement money. You just have to budget putting a portion of your earnings in the retirement plan to gain that benefit. Remember to pay yourself first. Often the money you contribute to these plans can be taken directly from your paycheck and are pre-tax dollars. That means you are not presently taxed on that money—an additional benefit to these retirement savings plans. A conversation with your banker, accountant, or financial advisor could provide other savings opportunities that may fit your financial goals. Many employers, if you work for a larger company, also offer free access to financial advisors to help you understand and meet your financial goals.

One of the underlying lessons to any of the seven principles is that it is never too late to start. If you have not been practicing sound financial principles, do not beat yourself up over past behavior. It is all about your attitude and committing to making positive changes now and moving forward.

If, this week, you did not save as much as you wanted, adjust those behaviors as you move ahead. Building financial security does not happen overnight. It takes planning, creating a realistic budget to include paying yourself first (savings), and managing your expenses. Financial freedom is when you have no debt, you own your home mortgage-free, and you have enough money saved to enjoy a comfortable retirement. That is possible for anyone who desires to achieve it if they follow the sustainable wealth principle. That's right, you too can obtain financial freedom—that's extraordinary!

Tips

1. Strive to master three basic tenets as soon as possible.

   a. Set a realistic budget.

   b. Fund a rainy-day account to cover emergency expenses. Try to start with $250 and gradually build until you are able to cover six months' expenses.

   c. Start saving for retirement by contributing a percentage of your income monthly to a retirement account and treat it as though you are paying a bill.

2. Create a financial plan. Whether you have the financial acumen or need an advisor to create a plan, a financial plan with realistic goals is essential. Reviewing and modifying the plan following any life change is expected.

3. Pay yourself first. More than a million people retire every day, and average life expectancy has increased into the eighties. Planning your financial future starts with your first job. Maximizing contributions to employer plans or setting up an IRA is essential. Many employer plans offer matching retirement contributions, which means they are giving you free money.

4. Live within your means. Never allow yourself to have buyer's remorse. Do not purchase items that require you to create debt or add to your debt if

possible. For example, a paid-off Toyota is much better than a Porsche with a payment.

5. Create a goal of total financial independence. This will allow you to enjoy financial resilience in case of unexpected expenses or volatility in your investments. Owning all your possessions, including your house, car, and luxury items, with at least six months of available cash on hand, helps to assure financial freedom.

6. Certificates of deposit (CDs) and money market accounts are types of accounts you can get at your bank that usually pay higher interest rates than regular savings and checking accounts for those not interested in investments with a greater degree of risk. Check with your bank to see if they have a financial advisor. Many banks offer free or low-cost financial planning to account holders. For those employed by an institution, access to a financial planner may be a benefit offered at no cost to you. Inquire with your employer's Human Resources department.

7. Learn how to save money while keeping a comfortable quality of life. For example, instead of going out for coffee every morning, make your coffee at home and put it in a reusable container. Not only will it save money but using a sustainable mug will help the environment.

8. Best practices for using credit cards to help build credit include:

a. Pay your bills on time, which is the single greatest factor influencing your credit score.

b. Pay the balance in full each month if possible. Carrying a balance does not help your credit score, although some people believe it does. If you can't pay in full, try paying more than just the minimum payment. The longer you have a balance, the more money you accrue in interest and the more debt grows.

c. Keep your balances below 30 percent of your limit. This applies to balances on individual cards. Not using all your available credit enhances your credit score.

Matters of Fact

- One out of three Americans has no retirement savings.[34]
- An estimated thirty-eight million Americans live paycheck to paycheck.[35]
- A full 93 percent of Americans have access to a 401(k), and only 67 percent of those who do make full use of matching employer funds.[36]
- If you start retirement savings at forty-five, you will have to save three times as much each month to retire as someone who started at age twenty-five.[37]
- Simple ways to convert spending into savings include packing a lunch for work, buying generic brands at the grocery store, and skipping the coffee shop. Put

the money you normally would have spent on these items into a savings account.[38]

- You shouldn't depend on Social Security for your retirement. According to a 2016 report by the Social Security Board of Trustees, Social Security is currently funded until 2034. After that, the program will be three-quarters funded. What that means for those retiring after 2034 is anyone's guess.[39]

- A 2019 poll by Bankrate.com found that, on average, Americans incur $3,500 of unexpected expenses a year.[40]

- From 1923–2016, the average rate of return on stocks from Standard and Poor's 500 most stable and largest companies has been 12 percent.[41]

- AP News Service reported that the Tax Code of the United States is approximately 3.8 million words long. That is three million words longer than the Bible. On top of that, tax laws change every year.[42]

- The average American annually pays $855 in credit card interest and $895 in car loan interest.[43]

PRINCIPLE FIVE:

Spiritual Core

Believe in something larger than yourself.

> *"We are not human beings having a spiritual experience.*
> *We are spiritual beings having a human experience."*
> Pierre Teilhard de Chardin, 1881–1955, French
> philosopher, Jesuit priest, paleontologist, and geologist
> who took part in the discovery of the Peking Man.

Look at the period at the end of this sentence. From our perspective, the dot is a static blip resting on a piece of paper or an e-reader screen, but there are literally zillions of subatomic interactions happening within the boundaries of that black circle. In the world of quantum mechanics, particles smaller than atoms can tunnel through barriers as if they didn't exist. The quantum world gets even weirder. When two particles physically interact with each other, they become linked. What happens to one particle instantly affects what happens to the other particle. Even if these entangled particles are light-years apart, the effects are instant. Einstein called the reaction of entangled particles "spooky action at a distance." I do not think it's spooky at all.

There is a common thread sewn into the fabric of the universe that connects everything. Entangled quantum particles are just one example of that connectedness. Anecdotal examples of underlying connectivity abound in the hard and social sciences alike. The French sociologist Émile Durkheim coined the term "collective consciousness" in 1893 to describe the interconnectivity amongst people. Collective consciousness is usually described as a fundamental force in society that is comprised of shared beliefs, ideas, and moral attitudes. Psychoanalyst Carl Jung modified that theory somewhat with what he called a "collective unconscious." Jung thought there was a genetic memory or near-mystical bond that creates certain patterns in society. Think about a time you visited the grocery store and walked past empty checkout lines. Isn't it always the case that, by the time you finish your shopping, everyone else in the store has also? The once-empty checkouts are now backed up three people deep. How or why did everyone stop shopping at the same time? Jung would say that it is the interconnectivity of our collective unconscious at work.

The concept of having a spiritual core starts with recognizing all of humanity's interconnectivity. How we treat others and ourselves has far-reaching implications that we may never see. While I'm writing this chapter, we are in the midst of the worldwide COVID-19 pandemic. We are living history in the making and what I'm seeing and experiencing is extraordinary. People throughout the country are shopping for at-risk persons, sewing masks, and making sacrifices to keep their communities safe. This crisis has underpinned how our actions toward others can literally be lifesaving. A kind word, a human gesture, or a charitable act can have an exponential effect. Joy and good tidings are as infectious as any disease, so small acts can change the moods of a multitude of people.

Understanding your connectivity to others and acting for the good of your fellow man is difficult, if not impossible, to do until you first center your own mind and spirit. Take the artist Shabazz Larkin, who was mired in a spiritual crisis. The one-time Madison Avenue ad executive directed the public's perception of products Americans purchase every day.

> One morning I woke up, and I was feeling worthless. . . . I didn't think there was a point to making art or trying to make anything for that matter. I thought to myself, I'm just worthless. I've got nothing to share. And then I feel like I heard God speak to me. And God said, "Ha-Ha! You are gold." So, I wrote that on a mirror.[44]

Larkin's experience motivated him to make amazingly simple pieces of art that feature messages from God. These pieces are commonly just a rectangle enclosing a saying signed by the Almighty. Larkin has dubbed this effort as *The God Speaks Project*. You can find him and his work on social media, but some examples of his slogans are:

- You are not who everyone says you are.
- No one can give you permission to be you but you.
- You are exactly where you need to be.[45]

The works of art started showing up in coffee shops, parks, and downtown Nashville's well-traveled alleyways. Larkin's is a story of how a man who quieted his troubled mind heard an inspiring message and reached out to help others.

The words or feeling you describe as God, goddess, the universe, the force, or however you choose to describe "the something" that Larkin heard doesn't matter in this discussion. Our discussion of finding a spiritual core has nothing to do with a specific creed, dogma, or definition of divinity. Whatever your beliefs, having a spiritual core allows for inner peace. There is no one answer or method for finding your core. But a good place to start is by asking these questions:

- Where do you turn when things feel hopeless?
- When it seems that everything is meaningless, how do you find meaning?
- What thoughts make you smile when nothing is going your way?

Some of us have a secure faith that endures from childhood and through one's family. Others will explore the traditions of the world to secure their own set of compatible beliefs and practices. Believing in something larger than yourself will prepare you for challenges that may seem overwhelming. Take the time to consider the deepest sources of your strength and nothing can defeat you!

When I was preparing for my first midterm exams in medical school, I studied every chance I had. My studying strategy centered around tackling the classes with exams earlier in the week first. I was taking microbiology that term, and it was one of my favorite classes. The microbiology midterm was the last one of the week, and I put studying for that class on the back burner. When you're busy studying, time moves fast. It was like I looked up from my books and the microbiology exam was already upon me. I quickly realized I did not have enough time to study as much as I would have liked for this class. I stayed up late the night before the microbiology exam to prepare. I looked over my notes and the texts until I decided I needed to get some rest. The next morning when I awoke, I made my way into the shower. As I stood there under the water, I realized I was certainly not as well prepared as I would have liked to have been. I did what any normal person would do in the shower the morning of an exam—I prayed. I asked God to assist me through the exam and promised it would be the last thing I would ever request of him. That seemed like a reasonable idea at the time. I clearly have asked for more from on high since.

That morning I took the fifty-question, multiple-choice exam as best I could. If you've ever had the "I didn't study for the exam dream," that's what I felt like. I put my pencil down and tried to put the exam behind me. The following week one of my good friends asked if I had seen the posted exam grades. I had hesitated to check them and told him I had not. He indicated that there was one person in the class who aced the exam, including the extra credit question that brought home a grade of 106. Surely that couldn't have been me. I made my way to the posted grades, and to my surprise, it was. I looked up, paused, and said, "Thank you, I owe you." I was a strong believer before and have been a strong believer ever since.

The microbiology exam is a true story. I tell it with a certain amount of jest, but I have always been spiritual. Having beliefs and convictions adds strength, character, and hope to one's life. I learned two powerful lessons from that first term in med school. The first is that it's okay to ask for help. When we have fought a good fight or simply fallen short of our own expectations, giving our cares to something greater than ourselves can give us the mental boost we need to overcome hard times. In many instances, like my microbiology exam, we have created these difficult situations for ourselves. Praying or asking the universe for guidance is a manner of self-forgiveness. One has to actively recognize the flaw in themselves that created the situation before asking God for a way out. Seeing our own shortcomings is the first step toward avoiding that pitfall in the future. Even if our prayers aren't answered in the way we want, we can plan to do better next time.

The second lesson of the microbiology exam is gratitude. This isn't the first time gratitude has been discussed in this text. Being thankful for what we have is key in any of the seven principles. We must recognize that our finances, relationships, or good health are given to us by our actions and seemingly random chance. Being happy with what we have been given and the opportunity to achieve more is the essence of gratitude. Don't curse your life because you didn't get a specific job or someone didn't go out with you on a date. Be grateful that you had the skills to apply for that job or the confidence to ask that person to dinner. When we focus on the good that is around and within us, bad days become trivialities. When we clear our minds of the flotsam and jetsam of negativity, we can grow in positive ways.

At our spiritual core, we cannot consume more than we produce. If we ask for good things to happen in our lives, we cannot view ourselves as an island. We must be mindful that we are the caretakers of those around us, even if they are not people we know. Imagine you've finished shopping at the grocery store and are wheeling your cart to your car. When you walked into the store, everything was going your way. You found a pull-though parking space, the produce looked fresher than ever, and you even found a heads-up penny on the sidewalk. But your revelry in a mundane shopping trip is shattered when you get to your car. The person who pulled into the parking space behind you has pulled so close, you can't stow your groceries in your trunk.

The likely reaction to such a situation is to get angry at the car's driver. How could they possibly have been so inconsiderate? You have a mind to leave them a nasty note telling that person exactly what you think of them and their driving skills. But the fact is, writing a nasty note would probably take more time than pulling your car up a few feet so you could get to your trunk. I have yet to meet a human who methodically plans to go to a parking lot and pull up too close to someone else's trunk just to ruin their day. Let's be mindful for a moment before we give the driver of that car both barrels on a Post-it note. They might be picking up a prescription for a sick child, and staying within the parking lines was the last thing on their mind. There are a thousand what-ifs about the driver, but what matters is your reaction. In that instance, doing nothing and going about your business could be a mindful, positive act. Leaving a nasty note could make someone else's bad day even worse.

It's easier for negativity to ooze from our brains and become a physical manifestation when we don't take care of ourselves. Given the emphasis I've put on giving and being part of a community, it would seem counterintuitive to talk about self-care. But the need to be thankful and generous is precisely why we need to speak about it. The first things we should be thankful and grateful for are our abilities and talents that allow us to help ourselves and others. I have always lived under the premise that God helps those who help themselves. If our needs aren't being met, we cannot help others for an appreciable amount of time without harming ourselves. Think of your psyche as a car. You can run errands for elderly shut-ins in your car. You can also run your kids to soccer practice in that same car. You can go hither and yon satisfying what everyone else needs in that car. But if you don't periodically change the oil, your engine will seize up. The friction caused by the lack of lubricant will fuse the pistons to the engine block, and your once-useful automobile will become a work of lawn art. When we don't take the time to do the things that lubricate our emotional health, we will eventually shut down and become useless to everyone—including ourselves.

Self-care is not about being selfish or overindulgent. Spending an abundance of your resources on yourself only leads to problems in your life. Think about having a piece of cheesecake after a nice dinner out. Every so often, a decadent dessert is a healthy treat. But eating a cheesecake a day will lead to serious health problems. Self-care is about finding activities that renew your passions and ignite your imagination. Those are the activities that give us a sideways grin and a slight head bob after we're finished. That activity might not mean anything to anyone else in your world, but you've taken the time to enjoy something that's all yours. Birdwatching, hiking, sculpting—the activity doesn't matter. What matters is that it brings you enjoyment and peace of mind.

It's easy to miss the larger point of self-care as it relates to spirituality. Maintaining and growing one's spiritual core is a physical act. Defining the parameters of spirituality or studying tenets of faith are necessary mental exercises that make up a portion of one's spiritual core. We might name introspections of this nature as being mindful. Having grateful thoughts or ruminating over our place in the universe is not enough. We must turn knowledge and intention into action to achieve any positive effect on ourselves and others. Consider the last time someone opened a door for you. You can have a grateful heart and appreciate the gesture without saying a word. When we turn our gratitude into the action of speaking our thanks to the person who opened that door, that praise reinforces their good behavior and gives the person a positive mental boost. We can never say thank you enough to those around us. The more we practice gratitude as a mindful act of self-care, the more we create a nurturing environment where those around us are focused on the group's growth. That is truly extraordinary!

If gratitude is an area you need to develop in your life, here are some ways to turn mindfulness into a habit:

- Maintain a gratitude journal. Every day, write a few sentences about what you're grateful for.
- Start a "gratitude jar." Think of this as the exact opposite of a swear jar. Every time you feel grateful for something, put some change or a dollar bill in the jar. Once the jar fills up, donate those funds to your favorite charity or to help someone you know who is in need.
- Gratitude phone call or dinner. Once a month, call and/or take someone who has impacted your life to dinner and let them know how they have positively impacted your existence.
- Handwritten thank-you notes. In a time of instant communications, taking the time to send a real snail-mail card expressing your gratitude can make a huge impact on someone's day.

Being grateful isn't the only form of mindfulness that can be turned into action. Below is a list of activities that will help you practice mindfulness:

- Yoga
- Stretching
- Meditation

- Breathing exercises
- Nature walks
- Reading a book or listening to an audiobook

We need one of these activities to maintain a healthy consciousness. When performing any of these actions, you will de-stress both your mind and body. Remember, growth is nearly impossible when you shoulder a heavy load. Practicing these activities is sure to lift your spirits and set your body and mind on a path that will help you stay healthy and serve others.

Tending to one's needs is not limited to finding "me-time" activities. Self-care also means understanding your own limitations. Whether personally or professionally, there is only so much any one person can do. Sometimes you have to rub up against those limits to find out what they are, but an honest evaluation of what you are capable of is a form of self-care. Making sure you're getting proper nutrition and sleep is also self-care. Leaving untenable personal and professional situations is the most difficult form of self-care there is. Making a business profitable or a personal connection happy at your expense is an ultimate sacrifice of the soul no one should have to continuously make.

Our inner peace is disrupted when we aren't true to our nature. If you have a creative spirit and have a job that discourages creativity, you will not be able to find inner peace. Maintaining friendships with those who do not share your worldview will only fuel internal turmoil. The key to true inner peace is being honest with the people in your life about who you are and what you want. Think about the last time someone asked if you wanted to see a movie that you had no desire to see, but you went anyway because you didn't want to say "no." By the end of the movie, you were probably mad at yourself for not speaking up for what you wanted. Often, those feelings can turn into hostility toward your friend. Being genuine can be difficult, but there are mindful ways of expressing what you desire. When you were asked to the movie, you could have told your friend, "I'd rather not see that movie; let's do something else together." Expressing what you want is not always easy, but a tactful response will be better for you and your acquaintances in the long run.

Maintaining a spiritual core is a balancing act. We hold a duty to what we consider to be a higher power and to our fellow humans. We also have a duty of care for ourselves. There is no singular equation that gives everyone happiness. I wish it were as simple as creating a financial budget. On spiritual matters, sometimes doing nothing can be the way to start. However you wish to describe or formalize it, quiet, reflective time is a way to examine your place in the world. Many people turn to guided meditation as a pathway to self-examination. For others, a solitary walk in the woods does the trick. Whatever method works for you, turn off your cell phone and think about who and where you are. Then decide how you are going to make changes to find the balance between the things that are bigger than yourself and your needs. I promise that, with enough honest examination and tinkering, you will find the answers that bring you inner peace. That inner peace will bring happiness, resilience, and the fortitude to carry on your journey. That's extraordinary!

Tips

1. Think about how you see yourself and identify what is important to you. Choose the values you want to live by and how you can incorporate them into your daily life.

2. Believe in a greater being. This offers hope for developing oneself and gives strength during adversity and partnership in success.

3. Always be grateful. Count your blessings, as there is always someone facing a greater challenge.

4. Share your thankfulness with others. Never take any gesture for granted and practice acts of kindness. It can be shared with a simple thank you, a handwritten note, or a small gift of appreciation, like a $5 Starbucks gift card or other tangible symbol of gratitude. Remember that simple acts of kindness are always free.

5. Practice mindfulness, whether by meditating, praying, performing breathing exercises, doing yoga, or just taking some time for yourself to be alone and think. Clearing your mind with one of these techniques is like rebooting your computer.

6. Show empathy and compassion to others by understanding that your life experience might not be the same as someone else's story. People live their own realities, and we need to respect that.

7. Find your passion and purpose in life. The two go together. If you're not passionate about your purpose, perhaps you should reexamine it.

8. Set aside time every day to turn off your phone and shut out the rest of the world. You'll be surprised by how just a few minutes of uninterrupted silence can recharge your mental fortitude.

Matters of Fact

- Joint research from the University of California and the University of Miami shows a link between expressing gratitude and having a healthier life. The ten-week experiment tracked three groups. The first group wrote a few sentences about what they were grateful for each week. Another group wrote journalistically about their week's events. The final group wrote about what upset them that week. The group that wrote about things they were grateful for had fewer visits to the doctor, exercised more, and were generally more optimistic than their study counterparts.[46]

- Anecdotal evidence exists that shows gratitude and mindfulness increases self-esteem, improves sleep, increases energy, facilitates more positive stress responses, and decreases overall anxiety.[47]

- An informal study conducted by Thnx4.org tracked a group that wrote a gratitude blog for two weeks. The participants showed fewer headaches, stomachaches, sore throats, and less congestion than those in their control group.[48]

- The American Psychological Association offers a continuing education course called "What Are the Benefits of Mindfulness?" The class explores the benefits of mindfulness meditation as a tool for psychotherapy. The class concludes that meditation can aid in "self-control, objectivity, affect tolerance, enhanced flexibility, equanimity, improved concentration and mental clarity, emotional intelligence and the ability to relate to others and one's self with kindness, acceptance, and compassion."[49]

- The University of Wisconsin-Madison explored the question of "can we train ourselves to care more?" Their studies found that, with enough practice, feelings of love, empathy, and nurturing can become second nature to those who previously described themselves as having a hard exterior.[50]

- Joseph Chancellor of the University of California conducted an experiment at a Spanish Coca-Cola plant. Nineteen factory workers were tasked with making small gestures of kindness every day to their coworkers. The study found that after four weeks, there was a measurable increase in kind acts and happiness throughout the entire facility.[51]

- John Grubbs, PhD at Bowling Green State University, found that public opinion of the millennial generation, who have been thought to be entitled or narcissistic, has had an effect on millennials' beliefs. The reinforcement of this perception on social media and in the news made millennials feel that way about themselves, no matter their self-image.[52] Acting kindly and saying positive things does make a difference.

- Kenneth Hill, a psychologist at Saint Mary's University in Halifax, Canada, dedicated his career to studying how people behave when they are geographically lost. In reviewing over 800 search and rescue reports, he found that lost people feel a compulsion to move even if they have no landmarks or celestial navigation skills. The stories of these wandering lost people usually do not end well.[53] The correlation between having navigational guidance and finding one's spiritual core isn't too difficult to make.

- According to various sources, there are over 4,300 faiths practiced throughout the world today.

- You're not alone. . . In a 2016 Gallup poll, 89 percent of Americans believe in God or some type of higher power.[54]

Healthy Living

An ounce of prevention equals a pound of cure—practice daily.

"The doctor of the future will give no medicines but will interest his patients in the care of the human frame, in diet, and in the causes and prevention of disease."
Thomas Edison, 1847–1931, inventor and businessman described as America's greatest inventor.

It should be no surprise that a doctor would consider healthy living a key to individual success. You also might think that this chapter will be filled with target metrics for caloric intake, cholesterol counts, and other arcane statistics. Much to your relief, we won't be heading into that territory. You should be discussing those metrics with your doctor. My general approach to fitness is both simple and obtainable. I recently had cause to discuss my personal method with my doctor. During my annual physical exam, my primary care physician looked at my vital signs—my heart rate and blood pressure—after they had been taken by the nurse. He continued his exam, listening to my heart and lungs, smiled, and shared how good they sounded.

"Well, Gary," he said. "I do not know how you do it, but your physical exam and lab work look wonderful."

"You are not going to believe how I do it if I tell you," I shared.

My doctor leaned over curiously and asked, "What are you doing?"

"Eating healthy, exercising regularly, and getting a good night's sleep," I said with a smile.

My doctor and I both chuckled at my simple-sounding approach to fitness. Healthy living doesn't have to be complicated. A healthy diet, drinking plenty of water, exercising regularly, and getting enough hours of sleep are the main factors in health maintenance. Starting with these basics will give you a foundation for any other fitness goals you might have.

As a doctor, I wish that I could tell you that a healthy lifestyle will mean that you will never need to be in a doctor's care. Unfortunately, that is simply not true. No matter how well you eat or how much exercise you get, chances are you'll need to go to a doctor for more than just a checkup at some point in your life. What living a healthy life does give you is a decreased risk of comorbidities if something suboptimal happens with your health. It can also help you conquer illnesses and ailments faster and easier than someone who is unhealthy. Let's say, through no fault of your own, you need to have your knee replaced. The healing and recovery process will likely be quicker and less painful if you maintained a good fitness level before your surgery.

A healthy lifestyle also allows us to be active and engaged with the world around us. In one's youth, it's difficult to see yourself using a walker or being unable to keep up with your children or grandchildren. Part of living an extraordinary life is seeing the roads ahead of us and planning for likely eventualities. As we age, our bodies lose muscle mass, and our energy levels decline. A healthy and active lifestyle combats the effects of aging. That doesn't mean that you'll necessarily be able to run a marathon when you're sixty, although you might. But you will have a better chance of chasing after a three-year-old grandchild darting around a playground and being active for longer in your life. We need to keep moving so we don't stop moving!

The good news is that it is never too late to adopt healthy habits. The advice in this chapter applies to anyone of any age. Everyone is different and should seek the counsel of their own physician before making major lifestyle changes. Even when making positive changes, talk with your doctor about the best way to get to where you want to be, given your individual medical history. With proper medical oversight, our bodies are amazing machines that can repair themselves with a little help from their operators. Consider someone who has smoked for ten or more years and quits. Two weeks after that person's last cigarette, their lung function can increase by as much as 30 percent.[55] One hundred and fifty minutes of brisk walking a week can reduce your chances of heart disease, obesity, diabetes, high blood pressure, and depression.[56] A little exercise can go a long way toward improving your health at any age.

You don't have to convince Texan real estate magnate Tom Thompson that an active life leads to extraordinary things. Tom played high school football, but due to a series of events, he was never able to play at a collegiate level. Still, Tom never gave up on his dream of finishing college and dressing out to take the field. At various times in his adult life, Tom tried to walk onto various professional and semiprofessional football teams, but nothing ever panned out there either. The rejections and missed chances didn't deter Tom from staying fit, though. He earned his black belt in karate on his path toward never being sedentary. Life is funny sometimes, and Tom went back to college and did make the football team. He now holds the record for being the oldest player to score in an NCAA football game. Tom Thompson kicked an extra point for the Austin College Kangaroos when he was sixty-one years old.[57] That's extraordinary.

Tom recognized that maintaining fitness throughout one's adult life isn't about boot-camp-style workouts or keeping up with fitness idols on social media. Fitness is about finding an activity that you enjoy doing that isn't a chore. Tom's primary physical outlet, martial arts, allowed him to hone his endurance, flexibility, and muscle strength. Most importantly, Tom got a sense of satisfaction from participating in karate. You could get similar benefits from working in the yard. If you've ever pulled weeds or planted shrubs for an afternoon, you might have wished you'd just gone to the gym instead. But if you enjoy gardening, go for it. Find something that is fun for you, whether it is part of a team sport or going for a run or bicycle ride. Involving a friend or significant other can make your physical activity more fulfilling. You and an activity partner can turn exercise into a social event that's a little more fun than working out on your own. Whatever keeps you moving and happy is the way to go. You'll be more likely to stick to an activity that brings joy and balance to your life than one that feels like yet another thing to do on your daily checklist.

There will be times when any fitness-related activity will feel like a chore and you will have tons of "those days" that will make your chosen physical activities seem out of reach. The wonderful thing about exercise is that aerobic activity releases serotonin and other endorphins into our brains. These neurotransmitters can lead to feelings of well-being and stress relief. Taking time out for physical activity on those horrible days will help. If you simply can't fit in a normal fitness routine, do some physical activity for fifteen minutes. You could do five minutes of push-ups, five minutes of jumping jacks, and five minutes of sit-ups. You could jog with your dog, pick up a game of basketball, or follow a workout video on YouTube. A few minutes of exercise on those hectic days will reinforce exercise as a fixture in your life. Striving for perfection every day does not have to be the goal. The goal is to keep fitness a part of your daily regimen. It's much harder to keep a fitness commitment if you're constantly stopping and starting a routine.

One of the most difficult fitness habits to fall into is sleep. One generally does not think of sleep as being important to a fitness plan, but sleep's overall effects on one's health are incalculable. Sleep is rarely thought of as a fitness component because exercise doesn't happen when you're lying in bed. In the last several years, however, sleep has become a topic of many studies that link proper sleep habits with increased mental and physical benefits. A Stanford University study of college athletes found that getting at least ten hours of sleep a night for seven to eight weeks improved the athlete's sprint times and stamina.[58] If you're looking to lose weight, sleep might be your secret weapon too. According to a University of Chicago study, well-rested dieters lost more fat than their study counterparts who didn't get enough sleep. The study also found that there was a link between the duration of the participants' sleep and appetite.[59] Who knows what sleep studies will uncover in the years to come, but the headline is about the value of getting some rest!

While studies differ on the amount of sleep one should get each night, seven to eight hours is a good mark to shoot for. Getting this much sleep a night isn't going to magically happen. You must create a life plan that will allow you to get enough sleep and exercise. Time is a finite resource that should be treated no differently than money. If you budget your finances, you can certainly budget your time to account for exercise and sleep. Once you have allotted your daily activities to allow seven to eight hours of rest each night, staying on your schedule will increase your chances of successfully getting enough sleep. Limit your caffeine and carbohydrate intake in the hours before bed. Having that midnight snack or cup of caffeinated hot tea will stimulate your body and make falling asleep much more difficult. If you're feeling parched before bedtime, grabbing a glass of water is your best bet. The National Sleep Foundation has found that going to bed hydrated can improve both the quality and duration of your slumber.[60]

Water consumption is not just something we should think about before bed. Proper hydration is as important to a healthy lifestyle as a diet. We're often told to "drink plenty of water," but rarely is it explained to us why proper water consumption is important to our health. Water is the foundation of every cell in our bodies. We would not be able to maintain our internal temperature without water acting as an insulator. Conversely, the water excreting through our skin as perspiration helps regulate our body temperature and removes some waste from our bodies. Most importantly, water is the body's primary solvent. Minerals, vitamins, and other nutrients are all dissolved using water. We couldn't metabolize food's carbohydrates or proteins if it was not for the ubiquitous building block of life—water. Believe it or not, our bodies' total makeup is 60–70 percent water.[61]

Your body ceases to function optimally if you are not properly hydrated. Dehydration is not a term that crops up on a random Wednesday at the office, but it should. Throughout the day, our bodies lose water through breathing, perspiration, and urine/bowel movements. It is possible to suffer the ill effects of dehydration outside of extreme or emergency circumstances. Losing 1–2 percent of your body weight from fluid loss is considered mild dehydration. Caffeine can be a contributing factor. Coffee, tea, and soda contain caffeine and deplete your body of fluids and contribute to dehydration. At even low levels of dehydration, you can experience headaches, irritability, and fatigue.[62] The next time you have a headache, think about reaching for a glass of water before taking aspirin.

With all our bodily functions relying on water, we must consume a certain amount of water each day. The question is: how much water should we be drinking? For years folk wisdom regarding water consumption has resulted in the "eight-by-eight rule." That standard maintains that an adult should consume eight eight-ounce servings of water a day to maintain proper health. Nobody's sure where the idea of drinking sixty-four ounces of water a day came from. Some say it was a guide given to soldiers during World War II. Others credit health and wellness books published in the 1970s with fixing the eight-by-eight rule in our minds. The eight-by-eight rule is a good starting point, but studies show you should be drinking more.

The National Academies of Sciences, Engineering, and Medicine recommends that the average male intake 3.7 liters of fluid each day and every female should intake 2.7 liters of fluid a day. That amount is significantly more than the 1.89 liters a day the eight-by-eight rule prescribes. Like any "rule" recommended by the National Academies, these figures are a guideline. Exercise, prescription medications, underlying health conditions, and the climate of where you live can impact your daily fluid intake. The good news is that you don't have to solely rely on throwing back bottle after bottle of water to hit your target. Any beverage you drink will have a high percentage of water as its base. Only 80 percent of fluid intake should be in liquid form. The other 20 percent will come from your diet.

This brings us to the topic of diet. Usually, whenever a doctor discusses diet with us, our instinct is to run in the other direction. The fear is that doctors want to curtail one of the most essential functions of our lives. Eating isn't simply about fueling our bodies and offering nutrition for the necessary activities of life. Mealtime socialization is as engrained in our collective consciousness as the need for sleep. Put simply, life happens around a table. We celebrate victories and discuss weighty matters over food. Holidays and remembrances are centered around a delicious meal. Whenever we discuss changing or limiting our diet, our mental resistance doesn't only come from missing out on sweets or cheeseburgers. The mental block we feel when anyone suggests we alter our diet is rooted in the fear that we will limit the activities associated with food as well. How could Thanksgiving possibly be as much fun without that third dessert? A romantic dinner just will not be the same without a plate of delicious carb-laden linguini.

So why is managing our diet so important, especially in our current high-tech society? Shouldn't it be easier? In days past, humans accessed food through hunting and gathering. High levels of physical activity were necessary for securing food and obtaining shelter. Our bodies' regulatory mechanisms adjusted to ensure sufficient food intake prevented the loss of body mass. Today, food is abundant, inexpensive, and served in large portions. Rather than hunting in the wild, a quick drive to the supermarket or a fast-food restaurant offers high-calorie, delicious, supersized meals. After the meal and a quick nap, logging back into the computer is easy. Who wants to get on the treadmill or go for a run? That can wait until tomorrow—or can it? This line of thinking has created an environment that promotes weight gain through a poor balance of food consumed and energy expended. Technology has made it easier for us to be productive without effort. Our ancestors wanted it to be easier but did not think of these consequences. Now a conscious effort has to be made to ensure a healthy balance. Small behavior changes can have a large impact on maintaining a healthy weight and feeling well.

Our relationship with food is all about our attitude. When food is used as a mood enhancer, a dangerous precedent is set. One may associate a feeling of comradery or kinship with the sugar high of a dessert. The term "comfort carbs" exists for a reason. When simple sugars are metabolized in our bodies, there is a feeling of euphoria that follows. If we come to depend on that little mood bump from any food or substance, we might start masking other problems in our lives. We run the risk of degrading our bodies and relationships over the very thing that is meant to sustain our physical and psychological health. If we come to Thanksgiving dinner for the food rather than for the joy of the company we will be joining, there is a problem with our relationship with food and/or those we are dining with.

If we extend the thought of food being a relationship, making good food choices is analogous to building a lasting interpersonal connection. Long-term friendships and familial bonds are built on boundaries, trust, and mutual respect. Our diets must be built along those same lines. We set boundaries with food by limiting the quantity and type of food we put into our bodies. If there is an issue with food or it has become a negative influence in our lives, then that history must be examined. Trust is built by choosing real food over heavily processed products. Think of fast food as a catty acquaintance you have who only likes to gossip. Participating in those conversations is never good for anyone. When we invest in good, wholesome food choices in reasonable quantities, our food will pay us dividends of a healthier, happy life.

Finding the right balance between exercise, sleep, fluid intake, and diet is what living a healthy lifestyle is really all about. If any one of these areas overshadows another area of your life, there may be consequences. For example, let us say you spent twenty to thirty hours a week at the gym. You might be on the road to the physique you want, but when would you have time for work and relationships? If you sacrifice sleep for extra gym time and diet radically, you may end up doing harm to yourself as well. Everything is best when it is done thoughtfully and in moderation. Finding the nexus point of health and happiness will give you the energy and drive to achieve these goals while ensuring there is enough time in your daily schedule to devote to other pursuits. Start with these four basic health habits as part of your normal routine:

1. Daily exercise.
2. Nutritious food with portion control.
3. Adequate daily hydration.
4. Getting a good night's sleep.

You will quickly observe noticeable results in how you feel from the minute you wake in the morning to the time you hit the pillow the following evening. That makes for a great, productive, and well-spent day. That's extraordinary!

Tips

1. Exercise and healthy eating should be part of your normal routine, eliminating the need for dieting or making special concessions to exercise, for example, as a New Year's resolution.
2. Stay well hydrated. Our bodies are 70 percent water, so drink at least sixty-four ounces of water a day to ensure proper hydration and water replacement.
3. Eat the right foods and manage portion size.
4. Be sure to get enough sleep to keep alert throughout the day and feel refreshed the next one.
5. Stretching, aerobic training, and weight training are all important. Stretching and aerobic training should be done daily; weight training can be alternated by muscle groups.
6. The Department of Health and Human Services recommends that adults get at least 150 minutes of moderate aerobic activity or seventy-five minutes of vigorous aerobic activity a week or a combination of the two. That's only twenty-one minutes of moderate exercise or eleven minutes of vigorous aerobic activity a day.

Matters of Fact

- Regular exercise releases endorphins that enhance your sense of well-being and can improve your attitude.[63]
- Sleep is not like a bank. The thought that we can sleep six hours a night during the week and make up for it with extra sleep on the weekends doesn't hold.

The human body isn't equipped with a mechanism to "save sleep" like fat stores calories for later use.[64]

- You start feeling thirsty when your body loses 2–3 percent of your body's water. One's mental and physical performance can start to deteriorate at the 1 percent dehydration level. Keep hydrated because you might see the effects of water loss before you even feel thirsty.[65]

- A paper published by Jianfeng Feng, PhD in *JAMA Psychiatry* claims a correlation between bad sleep and depression. His team found connectivity between the parts of the brain associated with short-term memory, self, and negative emotions. That explains why we sometimes lie awake ruminating over past decisions and lost love.[66]

- A 2016 study published in the journal *Scientific Reports* by Anika Knüppel of the Institute of Epidemiology and Public Health at University College London found that men who consumed sixty-seven grams of sugar from food and beverages a day were more likely to develop anxiety, depression, and other mental disorders than men who consumed less sugar daily.[67]

- Aside from the obvious benefits of exercise, regular physical activity can battle fatigue. Patrick O'Connor from the University of Georgia published findings to support this supposition in 2006. After studying 6,807 participants, O'Connor found that in 90 percent of the cases, a sedentary lifestyle resulted in lower energy levels and greater feelings of fatigue than a more active lifestyle.[68]

- Eating tomatoes, berries, avocados, nuts, and fish can help delay the visible signs of aging. Each of these foods contains vitamins that are beneficial for your skin. Berries, for example, are rich in antioxidants that aid in cellular regeneration. The vitamin C in tomatoes is a key component in collagen, which gives us firmer-looking skin.[69]

PRINCIPLE SEVEN:
The Art of Giving (Benevolent Arts)
Achieve the gifts of generosity.

"Gentleness, self-sacrifice, and generosity are the exclusive possession of no one race or religion."
Mohandas Gandhi, 1869–1948, Indian lawyer and politician who opposed British colonial rule of India through nonviolent means.

was twenty-nine years old and had just returned home from a two-week volunteer medical mission at a surgery clinic in Ahmedabad, India. Traveling home, I felt like I had a cold coming on. When you are going through airports and spending two weeks in a foreign country, chances are you'll come into contact with something your immune system has never seen before.

I did not think much about it, but my cough and slight fever dramatically escalated to a temperature of 105°F and I began to have difficulty breathing. I made my way to the emergency room, where they decided to admit me for further evaluation and treatment. The illness progressed to the point where I found myself receiving four intravenous antibiotics in the intensive care unit at New York City's Beth Israel Medical Center. Yes, I was a doctor—but *this* time, I was the patient. My training and expertise couldn't prevent septic shock from attacking my body. Fortunately, others were on duty who could oversee my recovery.

Thankfully, I did recover. The following year I was invited on the clinic trip back to Ahmedabad. I didn't even hesitate and answered, "Yes, of course! I am honored to be part of your good work." My family and friends were not eager to see me return to a place that had nearly killed me. Yes, there is a risk involved in anything you do, but I had to return. I had witnessed the desperate need in Ahmedabad and the tremendously beneficial effects of our donated time and skills. Our team of volunteer surgeons helped hundreds of people with facial deformities and changed lives in dramatic ways. The reward was worth infinitely more than the risk.

That's because charitable giving is an essential component of who we are as human beings. As we have previously discussed, humans are a communal species. It is because of our need to create self-perpetuating communities that we learn charity and compassion.

The act of raising a child or caring for the infirm can be seen as the evolutionary basis for giving. Our ancestors protected the weak and nurtured those who could not care for themselves. The young, of course, were nurtured to form the next generation of that community. The elderly were similarly cared for because they offered wisdom and guidance to the group. In nomadic tribes, it became a tradition to treat any traveler who happened upon the camp as an honored guest. Every major religion calls for some form of charity. Yes, giving is in our collective human experience just as DNA dictates our eye color.

In modern times, charity has taken different forms. Charity need not be on such an epic scale as allowing travelers a meal at your personal oasis. Charity can consist of small but impactful acts. It is always nice to give money no matter the size of the donation if one is able. In my earlier years, I always enjoyed giving small monetary donations. This was all I could afford on the small wages of a physician in training. To the person ringing a bell for the Salvation Army, I would give a few dollars. I might buy a box or two of Trefoils and a box of Samoas from young Girl Scouts in their green uniforms asking me to support their mission. Even these little gifts offer a larger sense of pride in knowing you've contributed to an important cause. Remember, every little bit helps!

As you adopt the principle of giving, you can advance the effectiveness of your commitment by making three decisions.

First: Consider what arena you would find most interesting or rewarding to devote your attention and resources to. For example, are you interested in environmental issues? Or would you find it more significant to devote your attention to issues related to children? Or are you concerned with assisting migrating people, or veterans, or those in a particular region or country? Or specific diseases?

Second: Decide how much of a financial commitment you can make. Can you reasonably donate $10 a month or $120 over the next year? Are you able to multiply that number due to changes in your finances? Greater financial donations can come as you build your own financial success. Come up with a list of charitable organizations you want to support and create a budget for how much you can give.

Third: Decide how much time you can reasonably give in a week or month or over a year. If your work is seasonal, you may want to give less time when you are at peak employment and more time when you have gaps. Remember that donating time is as valuable as donating money.

Sometimes the opportunity to give isn't as structured and opportunities present themselves in unexpected places. Mountaineer Greg Mortenson traveled to Pakistan in 1993 intending to climb the world's second-highest mountain, K2. According to his book, *Three Cups of Tea*, Mortenson became ill and lost his way on the Karakoram mountain range. He ended up in the small village of Korphe. The villagers took Mortenson in and nursed him back to health. So taken was Mortenson by the poverty and illiteracy of the village, he returned home and founded the Central Asian Institute (CAI). Mortenson believes that the way to break the cycle of violence and misogyny in communities is through education. As of 2008, the CAI had built sixty-three schools, most of which are for young women. Mortenson was also awarded Pakistan's third-highest civilian award, Star of Pakistan, in 2009 for his efforts.

The details of Mortenson's *Three Cups of Tea* have come under fire over the past few years, but the CAI has still educated thousands in central Asia. We can glean a few things from Mortenson's tale. First, opportunities to give aren't always apparent. Secondly, the CAI's approach depends heavily on community involvement. The CAI trains people in the communities they support to become teachers and leaders. That means that the CAI may provide facilities and supplies for the schools they support, but the process only works if members of each community take time and participate.

The familiar phrase "time is money" is an effort to acknowledge that your time is especially valuable. We should make good use of whatever time we have on this earth. That means taking time to focus on your own well-being, family and friends, and other interests and enjoyments. It also means that giving your time is of significant value when applied to helping others. My son and I recently spent several hours volunteering at a Special Olympics event. We helped set up, handed out water during the hot day, and cleaned up at the end. This was a great way for us to donate time. We had so much fun cheering, meeting people, and simply being part of a community that makes a difference. Think about the cost to hire someone and pay wages for those hours of work. Beyond saving the Special Olympics the cost of wages, the whole community benefits when participating in activities like this. We make connections that mutually enrich everyone's life experiences, and we participate in strengthening our community. That's not to mention the level of self-fulfillment individuals receive when assisting others.

It's easy to think of charitable giving and volunteering as solely benefiting the recipients, but this is not true. In fact, the one who gives may also be receiving significant benefits.

What are these benefits to the giver? Social connection is one of the benefits of giving your time to improve the lives of members of your community. Even if a particular project collects food, clothing, or other resources for people at a distance, you can gain from the communal effort with other volunteers. Numerous studies have shown that charitable giving improves one's feelings about themselves, as it is innate to humans to want to give. It feels good and goes a long way.

Our attitude about giving has to be tempered by good judgment as well as compassion. Charity is not meant to give someone a sense of entitlement. Our giving should be designed to get someone on their feet to help someone in the future. That concept is commonly known as "paying it forward." Let's say you're at the gas station and see a car with a sputtering engine pull up to the pump. The driver tells you he has forgotten his wallet, and his car is running on fumes. Paying it forward would mean buying that person a tank of gas and telling him not to repay you. The only compensation you need is for that person to help someone out in the future. Paying it forward is as much about charity as it is about teaching. By assisting someone, we have given them an example of compassion when they may never have considered being charitable to someone else. If the chain of paying it forward continues, we will touch more lives collectively than we might ever have assisted individually.

A friend of mine volunteers at a rural food bank's quarterly mass food giveaway. The food bank purchases a tractor-trailer's worth of food and lines up the pallets in an abandoned warehouse's parking lot. Recipients stay in their cars, hand their vouchers to the director, and drive down the line of pallets. Volunteers place the foodstuff in the recipient's trunk or truck beds. The system is efficient enough for 150 to 200 families to receive supplies in just a few hours.

The first time my friend participated in one of these give-aways, he became disheartened. Many of the recipients were driving newer model cars, and the incongruity perplexed my friend. How could someone who was driving a car that was newer than his need a handout? After the giveaway had ended, my friend asked the food bank's director about the disparity. The director smiled and told my friend that the town's main employer had gone out of business without notice. Hundreds of people arrived to work one day to find the gates padlocked and their jobs evaporated into thin air. Over half of the people who received food that day were out of work through no fault of their own.

After finding out the rest of the story, my friend felt sheepish. These people had probably made good financial decisions—when they had jobs. There was also likely a small percentage of recipients who were "getting over on the system" that day. The fact that they were doesn't diminish or excuse the responsibility any of us have to give. We cannot live a life without giving because some would take advantage. If we have a strong spiritual core, we know those who are unde-serving will answer for their deeds—just as we will answer for ours. Take a moment in your giving to check your own moti-vations, prejudices, and intentions. If you use compassion as your guide, you will seldom go wrong.

Charity is designed to elevate and ennoble everyone involved. Our charitable works toward the down-and-out are meant to give them a hand up and offer stopgaps in extreme circumstances. My friend who volunteered at the food bank went back and held a class on resume writing, interview techniques, and career counseling for anyone interested. Giving the people of that community food fulfilled a short-term need. The resume class also helped some people realize they were skilled tradesmen. After having an employment rug pulled from under you, thinking of yourself as "just a line worker who doesn't know anything but their job" is different than seeing a list of skills on a piece of paper. My friend's charitable acts restored dignity and hope to a community that needed much more than a handout. When we give of our time, we should always look for opportunities to give others the tools of success. If the pay it forward principle is at work, those tools will be spread exponentially throughout the world. Talk about extraordinary!

When people open their hearts to generosity, it can affect everyone around them in striking and profound ways. Ben Cohen and Jerry Greenfield, founders of Ben & Jerry's Ice Cream, established an idea within their company called "caring capitalism." This grew strongly out of Cohen's and Greenfield's radical mindsets in the 1960s. Caring capitalism means just that: Ben & Jerry's understands that it is a large company and it can make choices to help people smaller than them. For example, they found a Native American supplier for the blueberries in their Wild Maine Blueberry ice cream. They used ingredients from the Brazilian rainforest for their Rainforest Crunch, and the profits benefited the forest's preservation.

Earlier, we discussed three criteria that can help you decide how to practice the art of giving. It's often difficult to find opportunities to give in a more hands-on manner. Here are some ideas for places where you can find an organization or group that fits your giving criteria.

- **Online**. The internet is the obvious place to start looking for opportunities to give, but simple web searches don't always give the entire story. Check out social media to see what the organization's volunteers are doing. Reach out to some of those volunteers and ask about their results and experiences. You might find that an organization does stellar work, but their model isn't right for you.

- **Your employer's Human Resources department**. Increasingly, employers are developing a culture of giving that goes beyond an annual day of service. Someone in your company's HR department likely either knows or can direct you to charities the company supports. Companies usually vet charitable organizations they support, and that can take much of the guesswork out of the process for you.

- **Your local chamber of commerce**. Charities often work with or register with your local chamber of commerce. Someone at the chamber will likely have personal contacts at charities operating close to home. There's nothing better than spending your time making your neighbors' lives better.

- **Offices of professional and semiprofessional sports teams**. Sports organizations support specific charities and love for their fans to become involved. Call the front office of your favorite team and ask if they have a line on volunteer work.

- **Social and professional organizations**. If you belong to either of these types of groups, there is a good chance good works are being done. Check with your club's president or secretary to find out how you can get involved.

- **Your local school board**. In the United States, there is one constant: public schools are underfunded and teachers face unprecedented challenges. Many school systems have homework hotlines for students who need help with assignments. Guidance counselors need people with real work experience to speak to students about career choices. The need in the educational system is great, and the work can be rewarding.

There's no shortage of charitable ventures for you to examine. If all else fails, be creative and do something on your own. Do you have an elderly neighbor who needs their shopping or yard work done? Could you set up a free library or blessing box in your neighborhood? The next time you take a hike or walk a public greenway, take a trash bag with you and clean up. You don't have to be part of a nonprofit organization to make a difference and practice the art of giving. You simply have to be mindful enough to do some good in the world. That's extraordinary!

Tips

1. Give time, money, or both. Choose which depending on your ability and availability.

2. Get involved in your community; join a club or religious organization with a mission to serve. It is enjoyable to give, and doing it with others enhances the enjoyment and impact.

3. Volunteering doesn't only have to be a solo endeavor. Have you considered asking friends, family members, or work buddies along with you? If you're single, volunteering also makes a great date.

4. Most life insurance policies allow charities to be a full or partial beneficiary. You can discuss the possibilities of leaving a legacy with your insurance agent.

5. The United States is one of the few countries that allows tax deductions for charitable monetary contributions. Speak with a tax professional to see if your good work will reduce your tax bill.

Matters of Fact

- There are 1.8 million active nonprofit organizations in the United States, so there's never a shortage of places you can volunteer.[70]

- If you think helping your community doesn't amount to anything, consider this: according to a 2018 report by Volunteering in America, 77.34 million adults did some type of community service that year, for a total of 6.9 billion hours at a value of $167 billion.[71]

- In a study by the *American Journal of Epidemiology*, researchers found, in a sample size of 2,682 men in Finland, those who donated blood at least once a year had an 88 percent lower risk of heart attacks than those who did not donate.[72]
- Anecdotal studies show that volunteering and helping others reduces stress, combats depression, keeps you mentally stimulated, and provides a sense of purpose.
- *Harvard Women's Health Watch* reviews research and finds that a growing body of evidence suggests that people who give their time to others might also be rewarded with better *physical* health—including lower blood pressure and a longer life span.[73]
- Individual giving does matter to nonprofit organizations. In 2016, 72 percent of the $281.86 billion contributed to nonprofits in America came from individuals.[74]
- Americans, on average, give 3.1 percent of their income to charities.[75]
- According to the America's Charities website, 71 percent of employees surveyed say it's imperative or critically important to work in an organization supporting giving and volunteering.[76]

Conclusion

*"The two most important days in one's life is the day
you are born and the day you find out why."*
Samuel Langhorne Clemens (pen name Mark Twain), 1835–
1910, American writer, humorist, entrepreneur, publisher,
and lecturer. Lauded as the father of American literature.

None of us remember the day we were born, but we will always remember the day we found out why. Hidden within the major milestones of our lives is the answer to the why question. As a matter of fact, there will be many whys in each of our lives. There will be a reason why you took a specific job or you partnered up with your mate. The seven principles you have been reading about create a framework for the whys throughout your life. Take a day you wake up not feeling emotionally positive. Maybe you drop your toothbrush on the floor first thing, the shirt you were planning on wearing is in the wash, and then you discover you're out of coffee. Before you walk out the door, you stop and take a breath. You are at a decision point. You can either let these small misfortunes that really are inconsequential in the grand scheme of life impact your day and those around you or you can sluff it off and see walking out the door as a reset to a great day ahead. Because of your great emotional intelligence, you quickly realize that you can easily clean the toothbrush, wear a similar shirt hanging in the closet, and buy a fresh cup of coffee at the local gas station for just a dollar until you have the time to go to the grocery store to replenish your home coffee inventory. You choose the sunny side of the street—but why? You know how and why attitude matters. You understand attitude is an internal emotion that reflects widely externally on the world around you, and choosing a positive attitude enhances opportunity. You use the attitude principle wisely.

Beyond learning the seven principles, it is necessary to actively put them into action to see results. For example, there is no benefit in knowing that finding or forming a community will promote personal growth unless you get off the couch and actively participate in group activities. Working out how much you're spending on interest when using a credit card shows you why it's a bad idea to carry that type of debt. Being disciplined enough to not use your credit cards frivolously or purchase nonessentials when you do not have the financial means makes understanding the why more meaningful. Putting the knowledge into action brings success.

The seven principles are also not meant to be stand-alone elements in your life. Each of these principles is meant to work in conjunction with the others. Imagine trying to be charitable if you put forward a negative attitude. Or you might examine an underperforming financial situation and determine you need a higher-paying job. If that's the case, you may want to engage with your professional community to see if there are next-level job openings or take some continuing education classes to make yourself a better job candidate. There are endless ways in which the principles integrate, and you should be aware of those possibilities. As an exercise, write the seven principles down on a piece of paper, a small whiteboard, or in the notes section of your smartphone. Next to each principle, put down what you want to accomplish, the date you will begin, and the date you will complete the goal. Some of these goals may be easy and quick, but then sustainability may be the aim as you enjoy your journey of practicing the principle successfully.

Additionally, the seven principles are not meant to be a progression of skills or ideas. They are interconnected in that there is a synergistic effect when one excels at multiple principles. For example, if you doggedly pursue education and self-reinvention, you are likely to be exposed to higher-paying job opportunities. The more income you achieve, the easier financial planning and increasing savings become, preparing for a possible emergency or securing your retirement future. Each principle feeds off and flows from the other principles. The art of giving does not escape that formula for the interaction between principles, and one might consider giving to be a unifying principle for oneself. Giving helps others, creating a sense of gratefulness, which offers well-being for you and those you aid. It helps to build on relationships and fulfills our spiritual core. One act touches many principles and offers so much for you and those around you.

"Why me?" was the question I asked myself the day I received the phone call offering the honor to be the invited commencement speaker. Rather than self-searching as to why me, maybe my inner thought should have been: why not me? It allowed me to share my seven principles to success with this graduating class and has blessed me with a more fulfilled life. It encouraged me to write this book, so I can further enlighten others to success. That is why! Now you have read the ingredients of the seven principles, so why not you? Anything is possible if we put our mind to it, put the seven principles into action, and become determined to make success happen. If we fall along the way, we get up and continue the journey. That is part of the learning process: examining the outcomes of decisions along the way and learning from them, both good and bad. No one says achieving success is easy. The first six principles either offer us a vehicle to give or a reason to be charitable. Building communities and developing connections cannot happen without practicing giving. Without the proper attitude and desire to grow in your spiritual core, the act of charity is a hollow act designed to impress others and offers no benefit. By managing our finances and maintaining our health, we can give money or sweat equity to causes that matter and enhance others. To truly embrace education, mastery of a concept or skill must be taught to someone else. When we meld all the principles together and attain lifelong success, that's extraordinary!

Call to Action

When ordinary is just not enough. . . try extraordinary!

Visit our website at:
WWW.O2E4Life.com

The website offers evidence-based information that supports
each of the seven principles. Our goal is to share this
information to provide insight on how to enhance
your life and enjoy lifelong success.

About the Author

Gary D. Josephson MD, MBA received his bachelor's degree with honors from the State University of New York (SUNY) at Albany and his MD degree at SUNY Downstate Medical College with Distinction in Research. He completed an otolaryngology-head and neck surgery residency at the New York Eye and Ear Infirmary where he was honored with the Resident Teaching Award and Turner Award for excellence in otolaryngology. During this time, he was the medical correspondent for a local newspaper in Manhattan with a readership of over 350,000. His column included health and wellness tips and facts to improve well-being. Dr. Josephson also completed a pediatric otolaryngology fellowship at the University of Virginia, as well as an MBA with highest honors from the University of Massachusetts, Amherst.

Currently, Dr. Josephson is the Chief Medical Officer at Nemours Children's Health-Jacksonville and previously held the position of Chief of Staff at Wolfson Children's Hospital. He holds academic rank of Professor at Mayo Clinic College of Medicine and the University of South Florida College of Medicine. He has received many awards for his contributions to the medical profession and advocacy for children. Dr. Josephson has been named in "Jacksonville's Best Surgeons in the City" and listed in "Castle Connelly" and "Best Doctors in America" year after year. In 2018, Dr. Josephson was selected for the Albert Nelson Marquis Lifetime Achievement Award from Marquis Who's Who. He is an active member of numerous societies and participates on many boards and committees nationally. Dr. Josephson has numerous peer-reviewed publications in the medical literature in addition to invited articles, book chapters, and a medical text he edited titled "Complications in Pediatric Otolaryngology." He serves as a consultant for medical equipment companies and provides expertise on surgical innovation. He has developed several instruments currently used in surgical practice today. Even with many administrative responsibilities, Dr. Josephson remains actively engaged in research, education, and clinical care. He is often an invited guest lecturer nationally and internationally. He has enjoyed volunteering for international medical mission trips to care for adults and children with facial deformities. Dr. Josephson was honored by his undergraduate alma mater and was the commencement keynote speaker for the graduating class of the College of Biological Sciences. His address shared the seven principles and how they pave a road to success. On a more personal note, Dr. Josephson enjoys nature, outdoor activities, and staying physically fit. His greatest passion is spending time with his wife, Patricia, a Jacksonville pediatrician, and their two children, Samantha and Grayson. Dr. Josephson and his family currently reside in Jacksonville, Florida.

Bibliography

9News. "'Don't Buy $19 Smashed Avocado': Melbourne Property Tycoon Hammers Millennials over Spending Habits." 9News Breaking News. 9News, May 14, 2017. https://www.9news.com.au/national/melbourne-property-tycoon-hammers-millennials-over-spending-habits/f1e61616-94c2-4fa4-aa07-49a33f7bf842.

Blank, Laurie. "11 Recommended Budget Percentages by Category." Well Kept Wallet, June 16, 2020. https://wellkeptwallet.com/recommended-budget-percentages/.

Board of Governors of the Federal Reserve System. "Terms of Credit at Commercial Banks and Finance Companies." Board of Governors of the Federal Reserve System. Board of Governors of the Federal Reserve System. Accessed January 19, 2021. https://www.federalreserve.gov/releases/g19/HIST/cc_hist_tc_levels.html.

Bond, Michael. "Why Humans Totally Freak Out When They Get Lost." Wired. Conde Nast. May 13, 2020.

https://www.wired.com/story/why-humans-totally-freak-out-when-they-get-lost/?utm_source=pocket-newtab.

Borreli, Lizette. "Why Donating Blood Is Good for Your Health." Medical Daily, May 18, 2015. https://www.medicaldaily.com/why-donating-blood-good-your-health-246379.

Branch, Ali. "1 In 3 Americans Has $0 Saved for Retirement." GOBankingRates. GOBankingRates, March 14, 2016. https://www.gobankingrates.com/about/press-releases/1-3-americans-0-saved-retirement/.

Campbell, Denis. "Loneliness as Bad for Health as Long-Term Illness, Says GPs' Chief." The Guardian. Guardian News and Media, October 11, 2017. https://www.theguardian.com/society/2017/oct/12/loneliness-as-bad-for-health-as-long-term-illness-says-gps-chief.

Charity Navigator. "Giving Statistics." Charity Navigator, June 12, 2018. https://www.charitynavigator.org/index.cfm?bay=content.view&cpid=42.

Clason, George S. *The Richest Man in Babylon*. United States: HijezGlobal Press, 2020.

College Atlas. "Statistics of a College Dropout." College Atlas, 2017. https://www.collegeatlas.org/wp-content/uploads/2014/08/college-dropout-2017.jpg.

Colvin, Carolyn. "Social Security Funded Until 2034, and About Three-Quarters Funded for the Long Term; Many Options to Address the Long-Term Shortfall." Social Security Matters. Social Security Administration, November 6, 2020. https://blog.ssa.gov/social-security-funded-until-2034-and-about-three-quarters-funded-for-the-long-term-many-options-to-address-the-long-term-shortfall/.

Davies, Janey. "8 Surprising Facts about Relationships & Love, Backed by Psychology." Learning Mind, August 27, 2020. https://www.learning-mind.com/facts-about-relationships/.

Degges-White, Suzanne. "Ten Things You Need to Know about Friendships." Psychology Today. Sussex Publishers, August 10, 2016. https://www.psychologytoday.com/us/blog/lifetime-connections/201608/ten-things-you-need-know-about-friendships.

Edison, Thomas A. "Thomas A. Edison Papers." The Invention Factory—Year of Innovation Series, The Edison Papers. Accessed April 19, 2020. http://edison.rutgers.edu/inventionfactory.htm.

Elk, Kathleen. "Only Half of Americans Have Access to a 401(k)-Here's How to Save for Retirement If You Don't." CNBC, March 18, 2019. https://www.cnbc.com/2019/03/18/how-many-americans-have-access-to-a-401k-and-how-to-save-for-retirement-without-one.html.

Engels, Coert. "We Are Born Creative Geniuses and the Education System Dumbs Us Down, According to NASA Scientists." Ideapod, July 15, 2020. https://ideapod.com/born-creative-geniuses-education-system-dumbs-us-according-nasa-scientists/.

Fradera, Alex. "Small Acts of Kindness at Work Benefit the Giver, the Receiver and the Whole Organisation." Research Digest, August 2, 2017. https://digest.bps.org.

uk/2017/07/04/small-acts-of-kindness-at-work-benefit-the-giver-the-receiver-and-the-whole-organisation/.

Fram, Alan. "WHY IT MATTERS: Taxes." AP NEWS. Associated Press, October 3, 2016. https://apnews.com/article/15bb8f7f9a2d4f5fb2911829b9079298.

Giles, Lynne C., Gary F. V. Glonek, Mary A. Luszcz, and Gary R. Andrews. "Effect of Social Networks on 10 Year Survival in Very Old Australians: The Australian Longitudinal Study of Aging." Journal of Epidemiology & Community Health. BMJ Publishing Group Ltd, July 1, 2005. https://jech.bmj.com/content/59/7/574.

Greater Good Science Center. "About Thnx4." Thnx4. UC Berkley, November 6, 2020. https://www.thnx4.org/about-thnx4.

Greenhalgh, Steve, and Peter Panepento. "Snapshot Employee Research: What Employees Think about Workplace Giving, Volunteering, and CSR." America's Charities, March 11, 2020. https://www.charities.org/Snapshot-Employee-Research-What-Employees-Think-Workplace-Giving-Volunteering-CSR.

Grubbs, Joshua B., Julie J. Exline, Jessica McCain, W. Keith Campbell, and Jean M. Twenge. "Emerging Adult Reactions to Labeling Regarding Age-Group Differences in Narcissism and Entitlement." PLOS ONE. Public Library of Science, May 15, 2019. https://journals.plos.org/plosone/article?id=10.1371%2Fjournal.pone.0215637.

Hackney, Anthony C., and Amy R. Lane. "Exercise and the Regulation of Endocrine Hormones." Progress in Molecular Biology and Translational Science. Academic Press, August 5, 2015. https://www.sciencedirect.com/science/article/pii/S1877117315001337.

Kynaston, Gary. "The Mind Is Everything. What You Think, You Become." Hammersmith Academy, August 16, 2016. https://www.hammersmithacademy.org/news/mind-everything-think-become/.

Harvard Health Publishing. "A Purpose-Driven Life May Last Longer." Harvard Health. September, 2019. https://www.health.harvard.edu/mind-and-mood/a-purpose-driven-life-may-last-longer.

Healthline. "Drink 8 Glasses of Water a Day: Fact or Fiction?" Healthline. Accessed May 2020. https://www.healthline.com/nutrition/8-glasses-of-water-per-day#TOC_TITLE_HDR_2.

Helmenstine, Anne Marie. "How Much of the Human Body Is Water?" ThoughtCo. Accessed January 19, 2021. https://www.thoughtco.com/how-much-of-your-body-is-water-609406.

Hess, Abigail J. "Graduating in 4 Years or Less Helps Keep College Costs Down-but Just 41% percent of Students Do." CNBC. CNBC, June 20, 2019. https://www.cnbc.com/2019/06/19/just-41percent-of-college-students-graduate-in-four-years.html.

Hess, Peter. "Psychologists Reveal Why It's Harmful to Keep Calling Millennials 'Entitled.'" Pocket. Accessed January 19, 2021. https://getpocket.com/explore/item/psychologists-reveal-why-it-s-harmful-to-keep-calling-millennials-entitled?utm_source=pocket-newtab.

Housman, Michael, and Dylan Minor. Tech. *Toxic Workers*. Harvard Business School. November, 2015.

Hurd, Sherrie. "Practicing Kindness Can Change Your Brain, New Study Suggests." Learning Mind. Accessed January 19, 2021. https://www.learning-mind.com/practicing-kindness-can-change-your-brain-new-study-suggests/.

Johnson, Holly. "Here's How Much the Average American Pays in Interest Each Year." The Simple Dollar, September 30, 2020. https://www.thesimpledollar.com/loans/blog/heres-how-much-the-average-american-pays-in-interest-each-year/.

Kensington Consulting. "11 Ways to Remain Positive at Work." Kensington Consulting. Accessed January 19, 2021. https://www.kensingtonconsulting.co.uk/blog/2020/02/11-ways-to-remain-positive-at-work.

Knüppel, Anika, Martin J. Shipley, Clare H. Llewellyn, and Eric J. Brunner. "Sugar Intake from Sweet Food and Beverages, Common Mental Disorder and Depression: Prospective Findings from the Whitehall II Study." Nature News. Nature Publishing Group, July 27, 2017. https://www.nature.com/articles/s41598-017-05649-7.

Lake, Rebecca. "23 Dizzying Average American Savings Statistics." CreditDonkey. CreditDonkey, February 26, 2020. https://www.creditdonkey.com/average-american-savings-statistics.html.

Larkin, Shabazz. "Larkin Art & Co // Shop." Larkin Art & Co. Accessed April 26, 2021. https://www.larkinart.co/.

Leonhardt, Megan. "41% percent Of Americans Would Be Able to Cover a $1,000 Emergency with Savings."

CNBC. CNBC, January 22, 2020. https://www.cnbc.com/2020/01/21/41-percent-of-americans-would-be-able-to-cover-1000-dollar-emergency-with-savings.html.

Lipman, Victor. "Are Women Better Managers Than Men?" Psychology Today. Sussex Publishers, April 23, 2015. https://www.psychologytoday.com/us/blog/mind-the-manager/201504/are-women-better-managers-men.

Maldarelli, Claire. "How Many Hours of Sleep Do You Actually Need?" Popular Science. Accessed January 19, 2021. https://www.popsci.com/how-many-hours-sleep-do-you-actually-need/.

Matthew Frankel, CFP. "20 Money Stats That Will Blow You Away." The Motley Fool. The Motley Fool, February 1, 2016. https://www.fool.com/investing/general/2016/02/01/20-money-stats-that-will-blow-you-away.aspx.

McGinty, Jo Craven. "98.6 Degrees Fahrenheit Isn't the Average Anymore." The Wall Street Journal. Dow Jones & Company, January 17, 2020. https://www.wsj.com/articles/98-6-degrees-fahrenheit-isnt-the-average-any-more-11579257001?mod=e2fb&fbclid=IwAR2oDOM5R8_afwwoCJ72XzDrmbKCWm3ZHvRjkV1ThDlu60HJATQ-e-EYvNA.

Milanowski, Ann. "Evidence-Based Mindfulness: What Science Tells Us about Mindfulness Meditation and Its Benefits," October 25, 2017. https://consultqd.clevelandclinic.org/evidence-based-mindfulness-what-science-tells-us-about-mindfulness-meditation-and-its-benefits/.

Money Tips. "Charity Facts and Figures." MoneyTips, October 5, 2017. https://www.moneytips.com/charity-facts-and-figures.

Mortenson, Greg, and David Oliver Relin. *Three Cups of Tea: One Man's Extraordinary Journey to Promote Peace—One School at a Time.* Rearsby: W. F. Howes, 2010.

National Bullying Prevention Center. "Bullying Statistics." Bullying Statistics-National Bullying Prevention Center. Accessed January 19, 2021. https://www.pacer.org/bullying/resources/stats.asp.

National Center for Education Statistics. "The NCES Fast Facts Tool Provides Quick Answers to Many Education Questions (National Center for Education Statistics)." National Center for Education Statistics (NCES) Home Page, a part of the U.S. Department of Education. Accessed April 19, 2020. https://nces.ed.gov/fastfacts/display.asp?id=16.

NBER. "The Effects of Education on Health." NBER, March 2007. https://www.nber.org/digest/mar07/effects-education-health.

Newport, Frank. "Most Americans Still Believe in God." Gallup.com. Gallup, January 14, 2021. https://news.gallup.com/poll/193271/americans-believe-god.aspx.

Ott, Tim. "How George Washington Kept Alexander Hamilton in Check." Biography.com. A&E Networks Television, February 19, 2020. https://www.biography.com/news/george-washington-alexander-hamilton-relationship.

Perfect Motivations, Inc. "Awesome Facts About Workplace Relationship." Perfect Motivations, Inc., July

18, 2017. http://www.perfectmotivations.com/awe-some-facts-about-workplace-relationship/.

Ramsey Solutions. "How to Save Money: 20 Simple Tips." daveramsey.com. Ramsey Solutions, September 3, 2020. https://www.daveramsey.com/blog/the-secret-to-saving-money?msclkid=98760b8286cb18bc1abe55b3367c3b-9f&utm_source=bing&utm_medium=cpc&utm_c ampaign=FPU+-+Non+Brand&utm_term=how+to+ save+money&utm_content=Saving+Money.

Ramsey Solutions. "Return on Investment; the 12% percent Reality." daveramsey.com. Ramsey Solutions, March 3, 2020. https://www.daveramsey.com/blog/the-12-reality.

Rieck, Thom. "10,000 Steps a Day: Too Low? Too High?" Mayo Clinic. Mayo Foundation for Medical Education and Research, March 23, 2020. https://www.mayoclinic. org/healthy-lifestyle/fitness/in-depth/10000-steps/art-20317391.

Rogers, Everett M. *Diffusion of Innovations*. New York: Free Press, 1995.

Shabazz, Eric. "If You Want to View Paradise." Vimeo, January 15, 2021. https://vimeo.com/304238032.

Sheva, Arutz. "Study: Older Adults' Perception of Aging May Be More Important than Chronological Age." Israel National News. Israel National News, June 9, 2020. https://www.israelnationalnews.com/News/News. aspx/281576.

Sleep Foundation. "Surprising Ways Your Hydration Level Affects Your Sleep." Sleep Foundation, January 15,

2021. https://www.sleepfoundation.org/articles/connec-tion-between-hydration-and-sleep.

Sloat, Sarah. "Scientists Finally Understand the Link Between Depression and Bad Sleep." Pocket. Accessed January 19, 2021. https://getpocket.com/explore/item/link-between-depression-and-insomnia-found-in-the-brain-reveal-scientists?utm_source=pocket-newtab.

Soma Blog., "How Much Does Laughing Affect Your Body?-Laughter Is Good for Your Health." Soma Tech Intl's Blog, March 14, 2018. https://www.somatechnology.com/blog/tuesday-thoughts/how-laughing-affects-the-body/.

Sparacino, Alyssa. "11 Surprising Health Benefits of Sleep." Health.com, March 1, 2019. https://www.health.com/condition/sleep/11-surprising-health-benefits-of-sleep?slide=03a3dd2e-d8af-4946-a033-587a9db-65b08#03a3dd2e-d8af-4946-a033-587a9db65b08.

Springer, Nikki. An Analysis of James Surowiecki's "The Wisdom of Crowds": Why the Many Are Smarter than the Few and How Collective Wisdom Shapes Business, Economics, Societies, and Nations. London: Routledge, Taylor and Francis Group, 2018.

Stanley, Thomas J. "Rich or Drive Rich?" The Millionaire Next Door, April 28, 2020. https://www.themillionairenextdoor.com/2010/07/rich-or-drive-rich/.

Thompson, Emmet C., and Christopher P. Neck. Get a Kick out of Life: Expect the Best of Your Body, Mind, and Soul at Any Age. Franklin, TN: Clovercroft Publishing, 2017.

United States Bureau of Labor Statistics. "Number of Jobs, Labor Market Experience, and Earnings Growth: Results from a National Longitudinal Survey." Accessed January. 15, 2020. https://www.bls.gov/news.release/pdf/nlsoy.pdf.

United States Bureau of Labor and Statistics. *Employee Tenure in 2020*, September 22, 2020.

UnityPoint. "10 Reason Doctors Talk about the Need for Good Nutrition and Diets." UnityPoint Health. Accessed January 19, 2021. https://www.unitypoint. org/livewell/article.aspx?id=ff0de079-682c-4f1+a-b686-6b5b50e2f541.

University of Georgia. "Regular Exercise Plays A Consistent and Significant Role In Reducing Fatigue." ScienceDaily. ScienceDaily, November 8, 2006. https://www.science-daily.com/releases/2006/11/061101151005.htm.

University of Michigan Health System, Tobacco Consultation Service. "Changes Your Body Goes Through When You Quit Smoking." University of Michigan Health System, Tobacco Consultation Service. Regents of the University of Michigan, 2005. https://hr.umich.edu/sites/default/files/tcs-changes.pdf.

Vanlint, Nicola. "The Positive Benefits of Creativity." Life Labs. Kelsey Media, February 16, 2019. https://lifelabs. psychologies.co.uk/posts/4292-the-positive-benefits-of-creativity.

Volunteer Hub. "25 Volunteer Statistics That Will Blow Your Mind." VolunteerHub, July 14, 2020. https://www. volunteerhub.com/blog/25-volunteer-statistics/.

Western Governors University. "How Much More Can You Earn with a Bachelor's Degree?" Western Governors University. Western Governors University, October 16, 2020. https://www.wgu.edu/blog/value-bachelors-degree1812.html.

Yapp, Robin. "Friends Who Last a Lifetime." Daily Mail Online. Associated Newspapers, November 28, 2003. https://www.dailymail.co.uk/femail/article-202987/Friends-lifetime.html.

Endnotes

1   National Bullying Prevention Center. "Bullying Statistics." Bullying Statistics—National Bullying Prevention Center. Accessed January 19, 2021. https://www.pacer.org/bullying/resources/stats.asp.

2   Soma Blog., "How Much Does Laughing Affect Your Body? - Laughter Is Good for Your Health." Soma Tech Intl's Blog, March 14, 2018. https://www.somatechnology.com/blog/tuesday-thoughts/how-laughing-affects-the-body/.

3   Kensington Consulting. "11 Ways to Remain Positive at Work." Kensington Consulting. Accessed January 19, 2021. https://www.kensingtonconsulting.co.uk/blog/2020/02/11-ways-to-remain-positive-at-work.

4   Kynaston, Gary. "The Mind Is Everything. What You Think, You Become." Hammersmith Academy, August 16, 2016. https://www.hammersmithacademy.org/news/mind-everything-think-become/.

5   Sheva, Arutz. "Study: Older Adults' Perception of Aging
    May Be More Important than Chronological Age."
    Israel National News. Israel National News, June 9,
    2020. https://www.israelnationalnews.com/News/News.
    aspx/281576.

6   Engels, Coert. "We Are Born Creative Geniuses and the
    Education System Dumbs Us Ddown, According to NASA
    Scientists." Ideapod, July 15, 2020. https://ideapod.com/
    born-creative-geniuses-education-system-dumbs-us-
    according-nasa-scientists/.

7   United States Bureau of Labor and Statistics. *Employee
    Tenure in 2020*, September 22, 2020.

8   United States Bureau of Labor Statistics. "Number of
    Jobs, Labor Market Experience, and Earnings Growth:
    Results from a National Longitudinal Survey." Accessed
    January. 15, 2020. https://www.bls.gov/news.release/
    pdf/nlsoy.pdf.

9   Vanlint, Nicola. "The Positive Benefits of Creativity."
    Life Labs. Kelsey Media, February 16, 2019. https://
    lifelabs.psychologies.co.uk/posts/4292-the-positive-
    benefits-of-creativity.

10 NBER. "The Effects of Education on Health." NBER,
    March 2007. https://www.nber.org/digest/mar07/
    effects-education-health.

11 McGinty, Jo Craven. "98.6 Degrees Fahrenheit Isn't the
    Average Anymore." The Wall Street Journal. Dow Jones
    & Company, January 17, 2020. https://www.wsj.com/
    articles/98-6-degrees-fahrenheit-isnt-the-average-any-
    more-11579257001?mod=e2fb&fbclid=IwAR2o-

DOM5R8_afwwoCJ72XzDrmbKCWm3ZHvRjkV1Th-
Dlu60HJATQ-e-EYvNA.

12 Rogers, Everett M. *Diffusion of Innovations.* New York:
Free Press, 1995.

13 National Center for Education Statistics. "The NCES
Fast Facts Tool Provides Quick Answers to Many Education Questions." National Center for Education Statistics (NCES) Home Page, a part of the U.S. Department
of Education. Accessed April 19, 2020. https://nces.
ed.gov/fastfacts/display.asp?id=16.

14 College Atlas. "Statistics of a College Dropout." College
Atlas, 2017. https://www.collegeatlas.org/wp-content/
uploads/2014/08/college-dropout-2017.jpg.

15 Hess, Abigail J. "Graduating in 4 Years or Less Helps
Keep College Costs Down-but Just 41% percent of
Students Do." CNBC. CNBC, June 20, 2019. https://
www.cnbc.com/2019/06/19/just-41percent-of-college-
students-graduate-in-four-years.html.

16 Springer, Nikki. *An Analysis of James Surowiecki's "The
Wisdom of Crowds": Why the Many Are Smarter than the
Few and How Collective Wisdom Shapes Business, Economics, Societies, and Nations.* London: Routledge, Taylor
and Francis Group, 2018.

17 Edison, Thomas A. "Thomas A. Edison Papers." The
Invention Factory - Year of Innovation Series, The
Edison Papers. Accessed April 19, 2020. http://edison.
rutgers.edu/inventionfactory.htm.

18 Ott, Tim. "How George Washington Kept Alexander
Hamilton in Check." Biography.com. A&E Networks

Television, February 19, 2020. https://www.biography.com/news/george-washington-alexander-hamilton-relationship.

19 Campbell, Denis. "Loneliness as Bad for Health as Long-Term Illness, Says GPs' Chief." The Guardian. Guardian News and Media, October 11, 2017. https://www.theguardian.com/society/2017/oct/12/loneliness-as-bad-for-health-as-long-term-illness-says-gps-chief.

20 Degges-White, Suzanne. "Ten Things You Need to Know about Friendships." Psychology Today. Sussex Publishers, August 10, 2016. https://www.psychologytoday.com/us/blog/lifetime-connections/201608/ten-things-you-need-know-about-friendships.

21 Giles, Lynne C., Gary F. V. Glonek, Mary A. Luszcz, and Gary R. Andrews. "Effect of Social Networks on 10 Year Survival in Very Old Australians: The Australian Longitudinal Study of Aging." Journal of Epidemiology & Community Health. BMJ Publishing Group Ltd, July 1, 2005. https://jech.bmj.com/content/59/7/574.

22 Housman, Michael, and Dylan Minor. Tech. *Toxic Workers*. Harvard Business School. November, 2015.

23 Davies, Janey. "8 Surprising Facts about Relationships & Love, Backed by Psychology." Learning Mind, August 27, 2020. https://www.learning-mind.com/facts-about-relationships.

24 Lipman, Victor. "Are Women Better Managers Than Men?" Psychology Today. Sussex Publishers, April 23, 2015. https://www.psychologytoday.com/us/blog/mind-the-manager/201504/are-women-better-managers-men.

25 Perfect Motivations, Inc. "Awesome Facts About Work-place Relationship." Perfect Motivations, Inc., July 18, 2017. http://www.perfectmotivations.com/awesome-facts-about-workplace-relationship/.

26 Yapp, Robin. "Friends Who Last a Lifetime." Daily Mail Online. Associated Newspapers, November 28, 2003. https://www.dailymail.co.uk/femail/article-202987/Friends-lifetime.html.

27 Clason, George S. *The Richest Man in Babylon*. United States: HijezGlobal Press, 2020.

28 Blank, Laurie. "11 Recommended Budget Percentages by Category." Well Kept Wallet, June 16, 2020. https://wellkeptwallet.com/recommended-budget-percentages.

29 9News. "'Don't Buy $19 Smashed Avocado': Melbourne Property Tycoon Hammers Millennials over Spending Habits." 9News Breaking News. 9News, May 14, 2017. https://www.9news.com.au/national/melbourne-property-tycoon-hammers-millennials-over-spending-habits/f1e61616-94c2-4fa4-aa07-49a33f7bf842.

30 Stanley, Thomas J. "Rich or Drive Rich?" The Millionaire Next Door, April 28, 2020. https://www.themillionairenextdoor.com/2010/07/rich-or-drive-rich/.

31 Western Governors University. "How Much More Can You Earn with a Bachelor's Degree?" Western Governors University. Western Governors University, October 16, 2020. https://www.wgu.edu/blog/value-bachelors-degree1812.html.

32 Board of Governors of the Federal Reserve System. "Terms of Credit at Commercial Banks and Finance

Companies." Board of Governors of the Federal Reserve System. Board of Governors of the Federal Reserve System. Accessed January 19, 2021. https://www.federal reserve.gov/releases/g19/HIST/cc_hist_tc_levels.html.

33 This is Amazon's interest rate listed in their legal disclosures as of June 2020. Amazon may run introductory offers from time to time, but eventually, you will be paying 27.74 percent.

34 Branch, Ali. "1 In 3 Americans Has $0 Saved for Retirement." GOBankingRates. GOBankingRates, March 14, 2016. https://www.gobankingrates.com/about/press-releases/1-3-americans-0-saved-retirement/.

35 Lake, Rebecca. "23 Dizzying Average American Savings Statistics." CreditDonkey. CreditDonkey, February 26, 2020. https://www.creditdonkey.com/average-american-savings-statistics.html.

36 Elk, Kathleen. "Only Half of Americans Have Access to a 401(k)-Here's How to Save for Retirement If You Don't." CNBC, March 18, 2019. https://www.cnbc.com/2019/03/18/how-many-americans-have-access-to-a-401k-and-how-to-save-for-retirement-without-one.html.

37 Elk, Kathleen. "Only Half of Americans Have Access to a 401(k)-Here's How to Save for Retirement If You Don't." CNBC, March 18, 2019. https://www.cnbc.com/2019/03/18/how-many-americans-have-access-to-a-401k-and-how-to-save-for-retirement-without-one.html.

38 Ramsey Solutions, "How to Save Money: 20 Simple Tips," 2020.

39 Colvin, Carolyn. "Social Security Funded Until 2034, and About Three-Quarters Funded for the Long Term; Many Options to Address the Long-Term Shortfall." Social Security Matters. Social Security Administration, November 6, 2020. https://blog.ssa.gov/social-security-funded-until-2034-and-about-three-quarters-funded-for-the-long-term-many-options-to-address-the-long-term-shortfall/.

40 Leonhardt, Megan. "41% percent of Americans Would Be Able to Cover a $1,000 Emergency with Savings." CNBC. CNBC, January 22, 2020. https://www.cnbc.com/2020/01/21/41-percent-of-americans-would-be-able-to-cover-1000-dollar-emergency-with-savings.html.

41 Ramsey Solutions. "How to Save Money: 20 Simple Tips." daveramsey.com. Ramsey Solutions, September 3, 2020. https://www.daveramsey.com/blog/the-secret-to-saving-money?msclkid=98760b8286cb18bc1abe55b3367c3b9f&utm_source=bing&utm_medium=cpc&utm_campaign=FPU+-+Non+Brand&utm_term=how+to+save+money&utm_content=Saving+Money.

42 Fram, Alan. "WHY IT MATTERS: Taxes." AP NEWS. Associated Press, October 3, 2016. https://apnews.com/article/15bb8f7f9a2d4f5fb2911829b9079298.

43 Johnson, Holly. "Here's How Much the Average American Pays in Interest Each Year." The Simple Dollar, September 30, 2020. https://www.thesimpledollar.com/loans/blog/heres-how-much-the-average-american-pays-in-interest-each-year/.

44 Larkin, Shabazz. "Larkin Art & Co // Shop." Larkin Art
    & Co. Accessed April 26, 2021. https://www.larkinart.co/.

45 Larkin, Shabazz. "Larkin Art & Co // Shop." Larkin Art
    & Co. Accessed April 26, 2021. https://www.larkinart.co/.

46 Greater Good Science Center. "About Thnx4." Thnx4.
    UC Berkley, November 6, 2020. https://www.thnx4.
    org/about-thnx4.

47 Milanowski, Ann. "Evidence-Based Mindfulness: What
    Science Tells Us about Mindfulness Meditation and Its
    Benefits," October 25, 2017. https://consultqd.cleve-
    landclinic.org/evidence-based-mindfulness-what-science-
    tells-us-about-mindfulness-meditation-and-its-benefits/.

48 Davies, Janey. "8 Surprising Facts about Relation-
    ships & Love, Backed by Psychology." Learning Mind,
    August 27, 2020. https://www.learning-mind.com/
    facts-about-relationships/.

49 Hurd, Sherrie. "Practicing Kindness Can Change Your
    Brain, New Study Suggests." Learning Mind. Accessed
    January 19, 2021. https://www.learning-mind.com/
    practicing-kindness-can-change-your-brain-new-study-
    suggests.

50 Fradera, Alex. "Small Acts of Kindness at Work Benefit
    the Giver, the Receiver and the Whole Organisation."
    Research Digest, August 2, 2017. https://digest.bps.org.
    uk/2017/07/04/small-acts-of-kindness-at-work-benefit-
    the-giver-the-receiver-and-the-whole-organisation/.

51 Hess, Abigail J. "Graduating in 4 Years or Less Helps
    Keep College Costs Down-but Just 41% percent of
    Students Do." CNBC. CNBC, June 20, 2019. https://

www.cnbc.com/2019/06/19/just-41percent-of-college-students-graduate-in-four-years.html.

52 Grubbs, Joshua B., Julie J. Exline, Jessica McCain, W. Keith Campbell, and Jean M. Twenge. "Emerging Adult Reactions to Labeling Regarding Age-Group Differences in Narcissism and Entitlement." PLOS ONE. Public Library of Science, May 15, 2019. https://journals.plos.org/plosone/article?id=10.1371%2Fjournal.pone.0215637.

53 Bond, Michael. "Why Humans Totally Freak Out When They Get Lost." Wired. Conde Nast. May 13, 2020. https://www.wired.com/story/why-humans-totally-freak-out-when-they-get-lost/?utm_source=pocket-newtab.

54 Newport, Frank. "Most Americans Still Believe in God." Gallup.com. Gallup, January 14, 2021. https://news.gallup.com/poll/193271/americans-believe-god.aspx.

55 University of Michigan Health System, Tobacco Consultation Service. "Changes Your Body Goes Through When You Quit Smoking." University of Michigan Health System, Tobacco Consultation Service. Regents of the University of Michigan, 2005. https://hr.umich.edu/sites/default/files/tcs-changes.pdf.

56 Rieck, Thom. "10,000 Steps a Day: Too Low? Too High?" Mayo Clinic. Mayo Foundation for Medical Education and Research, March 23, 2020. https://www.mayoclinic.org/healthy-lifestyle/fitness/in-depth/10000-steps/art-20317391.

57 Thompson, Emmet C., and Christopher P. Neck. *Get a Kick out of Life: Expect the Best of Your Body, Mind, and*

Soul at Any Age. Franklin, TN: Clovercroft Publishing, 2017.

58 Sparacino, Alyssa. "11 Surprising Health Benefits of Sleep." Health.com, March 1, 2019. https://www.health.com/condition/sleep/11-surprising-health-benefits-of-sleep?slide=03a3dd2e-d8af-4946-a033-587a9db-65b08#03a3dd2e-d8af-4946-a033-587a9db65b08.

59 Sparacino, Alyssa. "11 Surprising Health Benefits of Sleep." Health.com, March 1, 2019. https://www.health.com/condition/sleep/11-surprising-health-benefits-of-sleep?slide=03a3dd2e-d8af-4946-a033-587a9db-65b08#03a3dd2e-d8af-4946-a033-587a9db65b08.

60 Sleep Foundation. "Surprising Ways Your Hydration Level Affects Your Sleep." Sleep Foundation, January 15, 2021. https://www.sleepfoundation.org/articles/connection-between-hydration-and-sleep.

61 Helmenstine, Anne Marie. "How Much of the Human Body Is Water?" ThoughtCo. Accessed January 19, 2021. https://www.thoughtco.com/how-much-of-your-body-is-water-609406.

62 Healthline. "Drink 8 Glasses of Water a Day: Fact or Fiction?" Healthline. Accessed May 2020. https://www.healthline.com/nutrition/8-glasses-of-water-per-day#TOC_TITLE_HDR_2.

63 Hackney, Anthony C., and Amy R. Lane. "Exercise and the Regulation of Endocrine Hormones." Progress in Molecular Biology and Translational Science. Academic Press, August 5, 2015. https://www.sciencedirect.com/science/article/pii/S1877117315001337.

64 Maldarelli, Claire. "How Many Hours of Sleep Do You Actually Need?" Popular Science. Accessed January 19, 2021. https://www.popsci.com/how-many-hours-sleep-do-you-actually-need/.

65 Helmenstine, Anne Marie. "How Much of the Human Body Is Water?" ThoughtCo. Accessed January 19, 2021. https://www.thoughtco.com/how-much-of-your-body-is-water-609406.

66 Sloat, Sarah. "Scientists Finally Understand the Link Between Depression and Bad Sleep." Pocket. Accessed January 19, 2021. https://getpocket.com/explore/item/link-between-depression-and-insomnia-found-in-the-brain-reveal-scientists?utm_source=pocket-newtab.

67 Knüppel, Anika, Martin J. Shipley, Clare H. Llewellyn, and Eric J. Brunner. "Sugar Intake from Sweet Food and Beverages, Common Mental Disorder and Depression: Prospective Findings from the Whitehall II Study." Nature News. Nature Publishing Group, July 27, 2017. https://www.nature.com/articles/s41598-017-05649-7.

68 University of Georgia. "Regular Exercise Plays a Consistent and Significant Role in Reducing Fatigue." ScienceDaily, November 8, 2006. https://www.sciencedaily.com/releases/2006/11/061101151005.htm.

69 UnityPoint. "10 Reason Doctors Talk about the Need for Good Nutrition and Diets." UnityPoint Health. Accessed January 19, 2021. https://www.unitypoint.org/livewell/article.aspx?id=ff0de079-682c-4f1+a-b686-6b5b50e2f541.

70 Volunteer Hub. "25 Volunteer Statistics That Will Blow Your Mind." VolunteerHub, July 14, 2020. https://www.volunteerhub.com/blog/25-volunteer-statistics/.

71 University of Georgia. "Regular Exercise Plays a Consistent and Significant Role in Reducing Fatigue." Science-Daily. ScienceDaily, November 8, 2006. https://www.sciencedaily.com/releases/2006/11/061101151005.htm.

72 Borreli, Lizette. "Why Donating Blood Is Good for Your Health." Medical Daily, May 18, 2015. https://www.medicaldaily.com/why-donating-blood-good-your-health-246379.

73 Harvard Health Publishing. "A Purpose-Driven Life May Last Longer." Harvard Health. September, 2019. https://www.health.harvard.edu/mind-and-mood/a-purpose-driven-life-may-last-longer.

74 Money Tips. "Charity Facts and Figures." MoneyTips, October 5, 2017. https://www.moneytips.com/charity-facts-and-figures.

75 Charity Navigator. "Giving Statistics." Charity Navigator, June 12, 2018. https://www.charitynavigator.org/index.cfm?bay=content.view&cpid=42.

76 Greenhalgh, Steve, and Peter Panepento. "Snapshot Employee Research: What Employees Think about Workplace Giving, Volunteering, and CSR." America's Charities, March 11, 2020. https://www.charities.org/Snapshot-Employee-Research-What-Employees-Think-Workplace-Giving-Volunteering-CSR.

A free ebook edition is available with the purchase of this book.

To claim your free ebook edition:

1. Visit MorganJamesBOGO.com
2. Sign your name CLEARLY in the space
3. Complete the form and submit a photo of the entire copyright page
4. You or your friend can download the ebook to your preferred device

A **FREE** ebook edition is available for you or a friend with the purchase of this print book.

CLEARLY SIGN YOUR NAME ABOVE

Instructions to claim your free ebook edition:
1. Visit MorganJamesBOGO.com
2. Sign your name CLEARLY in the space above
3. Complete the form and submit a photo of this entire page
4. You or your friend can download the ebook to your preferred device

Print & Digital Together Forever.

Snap a photo   Free ebook   Read anywhere